TOP SECRET

THE BOOK OF SPIES AND AGENTS

SOLEDAD ROMERO MARIÑO
& JULIO ANTONIO BLASCO

LITTLE GESTALTEN

CREDITS

TOP SECRET
The Book of Spies and Agents

ILLUSTRATED BY
Julio Antonio Blasco
WRITTEN BY
Soledad Romero Mariño

TRANSLATION FROM
SPANISH BY Emily Plank
EDITED BY Marilyn Knowlton
TYPESETTING BY Mike Goulding
& Little Gestalten

PRINTED BY Grafisches Centrum
Cuno GmbH & Co. KG,
Calbe (Saale)
Made in Germany

PUBLISHED BY
Little Gestalten, Berlin 2023
ISBN 978-3-96704-759-2

The SPANISH ORIGINAL
EDITION *ESPÍAS DE LEYENDA*
was published by
ZAHORÍ BOOKS,
©Zahorí Books, 2023
©TEXTS:
Soledad Romero Mariño
©ILLUSTRATIONS:
Julio Antonio Blasco
©for the ENGLISH EDITION:
Little Gestalten, AN IMPRINT OF
Die Gestalten Verlag
GmbH & Co. KG, Berlin 2023.

For more information, and
to order books, please visit:
gestalten.com/collections/
little-gestalten.

Bibliographic information
published by the Deutsche
Nationalbibliothek.
The Deutsche Nationalbibliothek
lists this publication in the
Deutsche Nationalbibliografie;
detailed bibliographic data are
available online at www.dnb.de.

This book was printed on paper
certified according to the
standards of the FSC®.

MIX
Paper from
responsible sources
FSC® C043106

4 PHILIP II

LEADER OF THE MOST ADVANCED INFORMER RING OF HIS TIME

THE SPANISH MONARCHY DEFENDED ITS POSITION AS THE GREATEST WORLD POWER WITH THE HELP OF SPIES.

10 THE FLYING SQUADRON

CATHERINE DE MEDICI'S INCREDIBLE NETWORK OF FEMALE SPIES.

22 MATA HARI

BEAUTIFUL DANCER IS ARRESTED AND EXECUTED FOR ESPIONAGE

THIS DOUBLE AGENT DAZZLED HER ADMIRERS WITH HER CHARMS AND DANCES.

36 JOAN PUJOL

THE DOUBLE AGENT WHO OUTWITTED HITLER

MUCH OF THE ALLIED SUCCESS IN THE NORMANDY LANDINGS DURING WORLD WAR II WAS DUE TO HIS ACTS.

40 NANCY WAKE

THE NAZIS' MOST WANTED SPY WAS A WOMAN

THEY CALLED HER "THE WHITE MOUSE" BECAUSE SHE ALWAYS ELUDED THEM.

44 ANONYMOUS INFORMANT

UNCOVERS PRESIDENT NIXON'S SPY RING

AN FBI INFORMANT REVEALED THE ATTEMPT BY US PRESIDENT RICHARD NIXON TO SPY ON HIS POLITICAL RIVALS.

14 RICHEBOURG

HE TOOK ADVANTAGE OF HIS SHORT STATURE TO CIRCUMVENT THE SIEGE OF PARIS DURING THE FRENCH REVOLUTION.

THE 23-INCH SPY

16

A GENERAL STAFF OFFICER OF THE AUSTRO-HUNGARIAN EMPIRE LEAKED INFORMATION TO THE RUSSIANS FOR NEARLY A DECADE.

ALFRED REDL
SPY AND GREAT TRAITOR

28 SIDNEY REILLY

THE LEGENDARY AGENT EXECUTED BY STALIN

AFTER CARRYING OUT IMPORTANT MISSIONS AS A BRITISH AGENT, THE FAMOUS SPY LOST HIS LIFE BECAUSE OF HIS OBSESSIVE FIGHT AGAINST THE SOVIET UNION'S COMMUNIST REGIME.

32

RAMÓN MERCADER
SECRET AGENT WHO ASSASSINATED TROTSKY

STALIN HAD BEEN PLANNING THE ASSASSINATION OF HIS RIVAL LEON TROTSKY FOR A LONG TIME. MERCADER BECAME HIS EXECUTING ARM.

50 THE CAMBRIDGE FIVE

DURING WORLD WAR II AND THE COLD WAR, FIVE SOVIET MOLES INFILTRATED THE BRITISH INTELLIGENCE SERVICE.

58

WOLF'S AGENTS SEDUCED WOMEN WHO WORKED IN KEY POSITIONS FOR THE WEST GERMAN AUTHORITIES TO OBTAIN CONFIDENTIAL INFORMATION FOR THE GDR.

MARCUS WOLF
AND HIS GROUP OF "ROMEO SPIES"

PHILIP II

LEADER OF THE MOST ADVANCED INFORMER RING OF HIS TIME

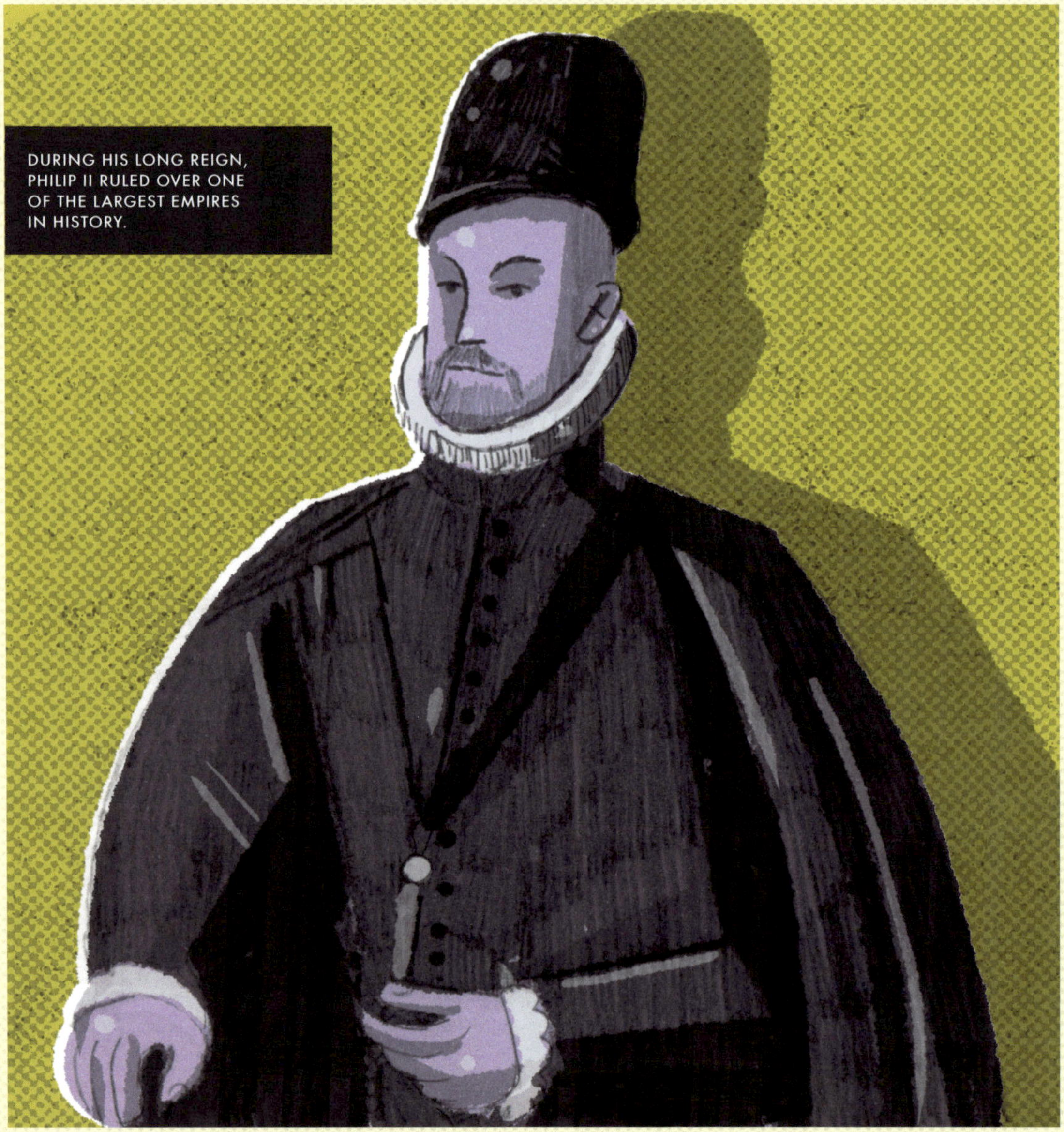

DURING HIS LONG REIGN, PHILIP II RULED OVER ONE OF THE LARGEST EMPIRES IN HISTORY.

NAME:
PHILIP II OF SPAIN, A.K.A. "THE PRUDENT"

BORN:
MAY 21, 1527, IN VALLADOLID, SPAIN

DEATH:
SEPTEMBER 13, 1598, IN SAN LORENZO DE EL ESCORIAL, SPAIN

SPY RING:
CROWN INTELLIGENCE COUNCILS

PROFILE:
AN INTERNATIONAL SPY RING DESTINED TO MAINTAIN THE EMPIRE'S SECURITY AND UPHOLD ITS POWER

CONTEXT:
PHILIP II'S EMPIRE WAS THE LARGEST GLOBAL POWER AT THE TIME.

AN EXEMPLARY AND METICULOUS KING

Philip II was the son of Charles I of Spain and Isabella of Portugal, and he was educated by illustrious humanist tutors. His father appointed him regent at a very young age, in 1543, when Charles I left Spain. This enabled Philip to experience ruling the empire before ascending the throne.

His reign lasted 42 years and was one of many military successes. He turned the Hispanic Monarchy into a major power of its time, with territories on every continent. He was also very meticulous, always requiring written reports from all his collaborators.

THE INTELLIGENCE RING SOUGHT TO KEEP SPAIN IN ITS POSITION AS THE WORLD'S GREATEST POWER.

THE FUTURE MONARCH AS A CHILD. PHILIP II WAS THE KING OF SPAIN FROM 1556 UNTIL HIS DEATH; KING OF NAPLES AND SICILY FROM 1554; KING OF PORTUGAL AND THE ALGARVE FROM 1580; AND KING OF ENGLAND AND IRELAND BETWEEN 1554 AND 1558 THROUGH HIS MARRIAGE TO QUEEN MARY TUDOR.

AN IMMENSE EMPIRE

TERRITORIES IN EUROPE

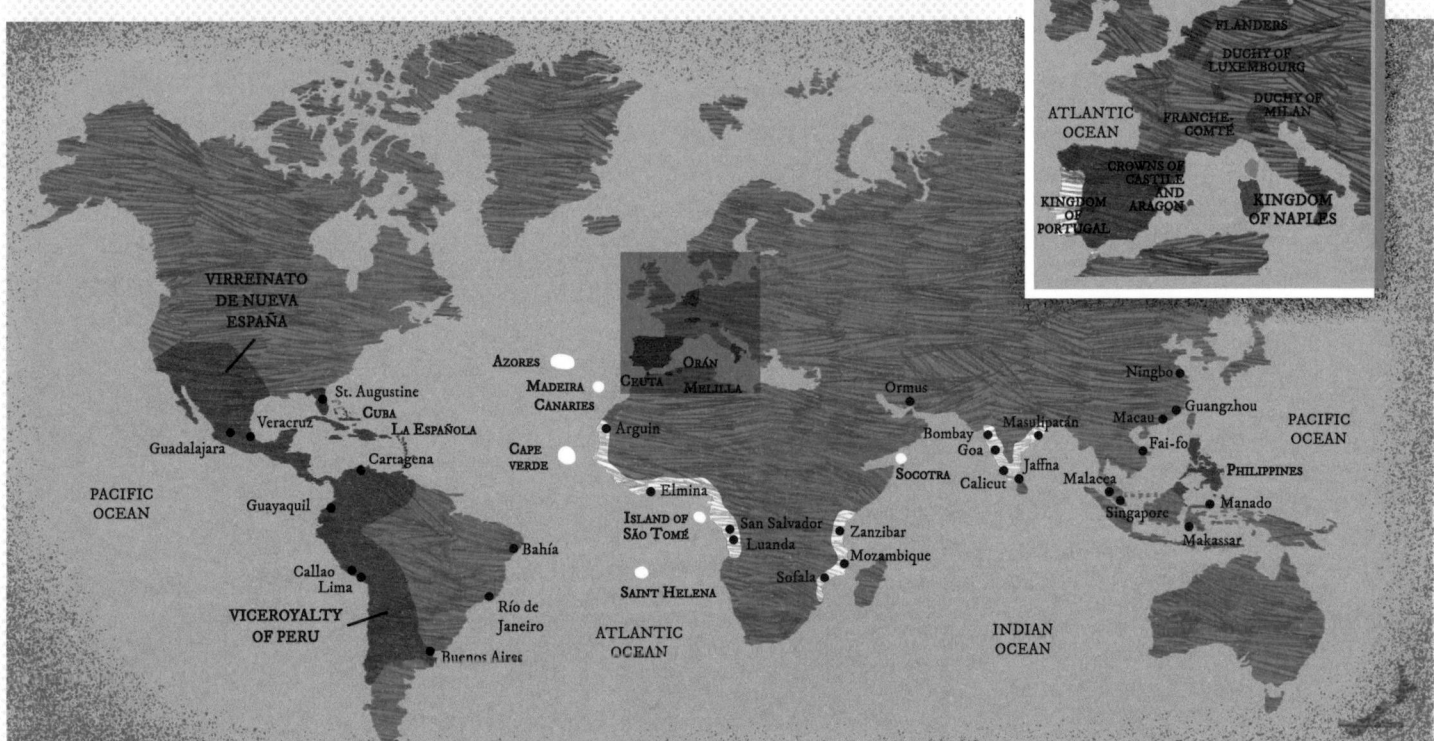

▬▬ PHILIP II'S EMPIRE PRIOR TO THE INCORPORATION OF THE PORTUGUESE EMPIRE

▬▬ PORTUGUESE EMPIRE, INCORPORATED IN 1580

● MAIN ESTABLISHMENTS OF THE HISPANIC MONARCHY

THE SPIES FORTIFY THE EMPIRE

Philip II knew only too well that maintaining the power and territories of his vast empire required more than simply having a strong army. Force needed to be coupled with information.

HIS INFORMATION SYSTEM WAS VERY MODERN FOR THE TIMES.

The king created intelligence councils to provide him with information quickly and reliably. He was kept abreast of everything that happened in Europe and in his domains throughout the world.

16TH-CENTURY SPAIN HAD A GROUP OF VERY ILLUSTRIOUS INFORMERS.

TOTAL CONTROL TO AVOID DECEPTION

Because of Philip II's mistrustful nature and desire to control everything, he appointed himself head of the Hispanic Monarchy's secret services.

Beneath him was the secretary of the State Council (with espionage capacities) and Juan Velázquez de Velasco, the royal court's greatest spy.

Philip II developed a process more effective than anything that had come before. The head intelligence officers were in charge of selecting the agents or informers and setting their targets. They also centralized the process for collecting secret reports.

HIS DIPLOMAT AND SPY NETWORK WAS THE GREATEST DURING HABSBURG TIMES.

EL ESCORIAL, THE CENTER OF OPERATIONS

The center of operations performed by the Hispanic Monarchy's secret services was the Royal Monastery of El Escorial, located in the municipality of San Lorenzo de El Escorial, northwest of the Spanish capital, Madrid. It was a vast palace complex constructed according to the orders of Philip II.

Completed in 1584, its royal palace was the coordination center for the various imperial intelligence networks. Reports were compiled on the identity of these networks' members and on the missions and position of each of the spies working around the world—on the Mediterranean coasts, in Northern Europe, in America, in Africa, and in the Pacific.

THE EL ESCORIAL COMPLEX,
COMPRISING A NUMBER OF
BUILDINGS—THE ROYAL PALACE,
THE MONASTERY AND BASILICA,
THE LIBRARY, THE PANTHEON,
THE COLLEGE . . .

CODED MESSAGES

Philip II wanted to make sure of one thing: If his reports were intercepted by the enemy, it would not be easy for them to be deciphered. The more complicated the coding, the longer it would take for the content to become known, and with a bit of luck, it would then be too late to act on it.

The king became an expert in using invisible ink in microscopic writing and in coded messages. His cryptographic nomenclator has been preserved:

PHILIP II HAD A CODING AND DECODING TABLE FOR HIS SECRET INFORMATION.

THE MOST EFFECTIVE MAIL SERVICE OF THE TIMES

Another of Philip II's notable contributions was the improvement he made to the existing mail service. The sovereign laid the foundation for the present-day system, and its network effectively connected Madrid to the major capitals of Europe.

IN ADDITION TO CREATING AN EXCELLENT MAIL NETWORK AND AN EFFECTIVE CODING SYSTEM, THE KING EMPLOYED "SPIES OF SPIES" TO MONITOR HIS OWN AGENTS.

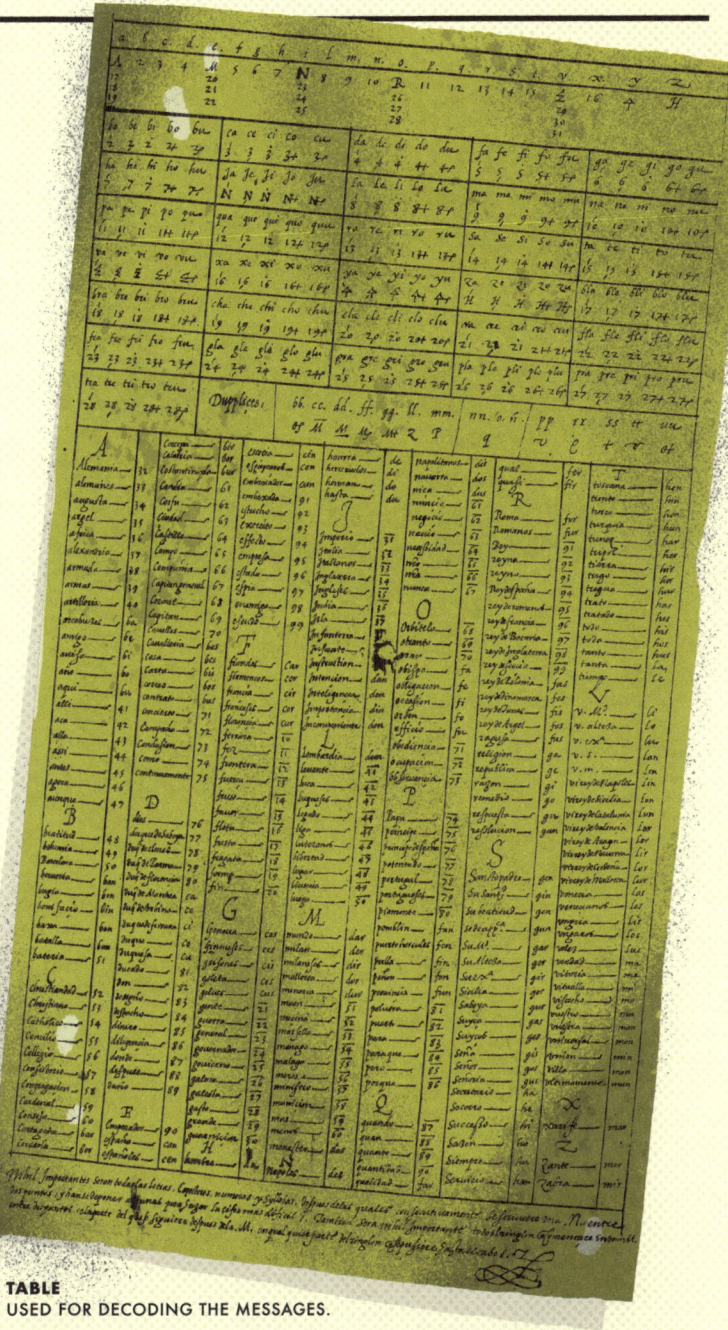

TABLE
USED FOR DECODING THE MESSAGES.

GOLD FOR THE SPIES

No other country at the time was dedicating such vast human and material resources to espionage. Gold from the public coffers enabled the Hispanic Monarchy to invest over a period of six months what England (its main rival in terms of espionage) would spend in six years.

FOR SECURITY PURPOSES, THE SPIES WOULD BE PAID FROM RESERVE FUNDS REFERRED TO AS "SECRET EXPENSES."

NOTABLE SPIES

TYPES OF INFORMERS

The king had civil agents and special agents, with the latter carrying out the more dangerous and more important missions.

1. "SLEEPING" AGENTS RING

These were spies who lived in European cities and generally led normal lives, waiting to be called up for a special mission.

2. FOREIGN OFFICERS

These salaried agents worked for other countries' governments, embassies, or armies in order to obtain information on military campaigns.

3. ARTISTS

These secret informers had contact with royalty and the aristocracy through their work. They used these relations to obtain information that they would then sell to Philip II.

JUAN VELÁZQUEZ DE VELASCO

MILITARY OFFICER

The kingdom's best spy was a Spanish soldier who played a stand-out role in several military campaigns and in key positions within the Spanish Crown.

His main job was to control the informers scattered across the continents and the information they provided.

He was also responsible for recruiting spies in England, Holland, and France, many of whom were diplomats, naval officers, soldiers, and monks. He was succeeded by his son, Andrés.

PHILIP II DECLARED HIM "SUPERINTENDENT OF THE SECRET INTELLIGENCE SERVICES."

IN RETURN FOR HIS TREASON, STAFFORD RECEIVED ONLY 5,200 DUCATS— A VERY LOW RATE FOR ESPIONAGE AT THE TIME.

SIR EDWARD STAFFORD

ENGLISH DIPLOMAT

One of the best moves Philip II made in his spy ring was to appoint Sir Stafford England's ambassador to France.

Sir Edward Stafford was a member of parliament and a very well-connected man, but he also liked to gamble and had serious financial problems. Selling state secrets to England's enemy helped him deal with hardship.

Stafford sold the details of England's military strategy for attacks, such as those the country made in Cádiz and Lisbon. He also betrayed his country by portraying King Philip II as a peace loving king with little ambition. In reality, however, the Spanish Armada was preparing to head to the English Channel to invade England.

THE SPANISH ARMADA

The Spanish Armada was Spain's fleet of warships sent out by King Philip II in 1588 to invade England, dethrone its queen, Elizabeth I, and restore Catholicism in the country. The fleet was made up of more than 130 warships and some 30,000 men.

The military operation was a failure due to various setbacks, the worst being bad weather, not the enemy's skill. As a result, the Spanish squadron was forced to retreat.

MIGUEL DE
CERVANTES

WRITER

The greatest Spanish literary figure of all time, Cervantes was also a soldier; he served Philip II in the Battle of Lepanto, and he was captured by the Turks and sold as a slave.

After five years in captivity, he managed to return to Spain, along with other prisoners.

A loyal servant of the Spanish Crown who was in need of money, Cervantes continued serving Philip II, who sent him on a secret mission to Oran, North Africa.

The king was able to make use of Cervantes' knowledge of the culture and customs in that part of the world, something that he had learned while imprisoned there.

At the end of his mission, the loyal soldier threw himself into the noble art of writing—a field in which he arguably rendered even greater services to his country and world literature.

PEDRO PABLO
RUBENS

PAINTER

An acclaimed artist, Rubens was born in Germany, but due to the religious uprising occurring there, he fled to Belgium with his family.

At that time, the Low Countries were under the rule of Philip II and the Catholic Church. The painter, a staunch Catholic, received important commissions from the Spanish nobility and monarchy.

Rubens was fluent in a number of languages and soon became one of the most famous painters among European aristocracy. Philip II made the most of the artist's good contacts and the information he was able to obtain. Rubens even managed to mediate as a diplomat between various royal courts.

PHILIP II HAD THE MOST RELIABLE INFORMATION IN ALL OF EUROPE.

FRANCISCO DE
QUEVEDO

WRITER

Quevedo was a Spanish writer, politician, and aristocrat during Spain's Golden Age. He was born with two deformed feet and was also nearsighted. He devoted himself to reading as a means of avoiding being bullied by other children.

Highly intelligent, he studied at Imperial College and then at the University of Valladolid, where he began to make a name for himself with his first poems.

QUEVEDO ALSO WORKED AS A SPY FOR THE MONARCHY.

He established contacts with great figures of European literature and renowned aristocrats. On a trip to Naples, the writer conducted espionage missions for Philip II.

INVESTIGATION

After his death, King Philip II was considered by some as a role model for standard conduct within authoritarian monarchies of the time.

Throughout his long reign—one of the most important in Spain's history—the king demonstrated the importance of having information on the enemy and affiliated countries as a means of controlling, conquering, or maintaining power.

PHILIP II'S REIGN PLACED THE INTERESTS OF THE CROWN ABOVE ANY PREJUDICES WHEN IT CAME TO USING HIS SPY RING.

GAZETTE

Paris, December, 6, 1591

THE FLYING SQUADRON

CATHERINE DE MEDICI'S INCREDIBLE NETWORK OF FEMALE SPIES

CATHERINE DE MEDICI WAS THE QUEEN OF FRANCE. SHE REIGNED WHILE HER SON CHARLES, HEIR TO THE THRONE, WAS A MINOR.

NAME:
CATERINA (CATHERINE) MARIA ROMULA DI LORENZO DE MEDICI

BORN:
APRIL 13, 1519, IN FLORENCE (FLORENTINE REPUBLIC)

DIED:
JANUARY 5, 1589, IN BLOIS (FRANCE)

SPY NETWORK:
THE FLYING SQUADRON, CREATED IN 1560

PROFILE:
A GROUP OF FEMALE INFORMANTS OBTAINING INFORMATION OF INTEREST FOR THE QUEEN. THE SPIES SEDUCED ARISTOCRATS, POLITICIANS, DIPLOMATS . . .

CONFLICT:
BETWEEN CATHERINE DE MEDICI AND HER POLITICAL RIVALS AT THE TIME

CATHERINE DE MEDICI

Catherine, the future queen of France, was born in 1519 in Florence, then one of Italy's most prosperous cities.

Catherine was the daughter of the aristocratic Madeleine de La Tour d'Auvergne and Lorenzo II de Medici, the ruler of Florence. In other words, Catherine came from a family that was one of the most powerful and illustrious in the Florentine Republic.

Just two weeks after she was born, her mother died of a fever caused by childbirth. Six days later, her father also died of illness, leaving the little girl an orphan.

In her early years, Catherine was raised by other family members, and she also spent time in several convents. When she was just 14 years old, her uncle, Pope Clement VII, married her off to the boy who would eventually become Henry II of France. The Florentine aristocrat moved to France, where she became part of the royal family.

CATHERINE MARRIED HENRY OF VALOIS, DUKE OF ORLEANS AND DAUPHIN (HEIR TO THE THRONE) OF FRANCE.

DURING HER TIME AS QUEEN OF FRANCE, CATHERINE DE MEDICI TRAINED SOME WOMEN AS SPIES SO THAT SHE COULD KEEP AN EYE ON HER ENEMIES.

SCORNED BY THE FUTURE KING

When Catherine de Medici arrived at the French court, she soon realized that her marriage was going to be anything but romantic. Catherine was not yet 15 years old and her husband, Henry II (also known as Henry of Valois), was more interested in his lover, Diane de Poitiers, one of the ladies-in-waiting at the court, than in his young wife.

Despite being 19 years older than the king, the very beautiful Diane was Henry's favorite until his death, in 1559. Catherine had to get used to living with Diane and with the humiliation this caused her.

DIANE HAD LOOKED AFTER HENRY SINCE HE WAS A BABY

The young Florentine woman learned something very important about her husband's lover, however. When a man falls for a woman, he becomes weak and allows himself to be influenced by her, freely revealing his secrets during moments of intimacy.

Later, when Catherine de Medici came to power, she would remember this lesson and go on to use it cunningly to her own advantage.

DIANE DE POITIERS

THE ETERNAL RIVAL

The beautiful Diane de Poitiers had always been the favorite of Henry, Duke of Orleans. However, the lady-in-waiting was fully aware that the future king needed heirs, so she made sure that he didn't totally neglect his wife. Catherine gave birth to 10 of Henry's children, three of whom went on to rule France: Francis II, Charles IX, and Henry III.

CATHERINE HAS A PLAN

QUEEN CONSORT

In 1547, Henry of Valois ascended the French throne. Catherine, the wife of the new King Henry II, became queen consort. She continued, however, to be excluded from power, while Diane de Poitiers maintained her political influence.

Things stayed unchanged until Henry II died in 1559 from injuries he suffered during a jousting tournament. Francis II, his eldest son, came to the throne at the age of 15, and Catherine began her rise to power as his caretaker.

Death dogged the family. In December 1560, the young monarch died after an illness. He was followed by his younger brother, Charles IX, who was only 10 years old.

Catherine ruled on his behalf as queen regent. For the first time, she could show how clever she was, and she wasted no time getting rid of Diane de Poitiers.

Among Catherine's arch enemies was Antoine de Bourbon, a French aristocrat married to Queen Joanna III of Navarre. To destroy her rival, Catherine quickly devised a

CATHERINE WAS NAMED RULER OF FRANCE AND ADVISED CHARLES IX IN MATTERS OF STATE.

plan. The queen formed a group of beautiful women who were trained to use their charms to seduce and control her adversaries. The group became known as the Flying Squadron.

TO COUNTER HER ENEMIES' POWER, CATHERINE CREATED A GROUP OF FEMALE SPIES.

THE SPY NETWORK

PROFILES:
To become a member, the women had to be attractive and swear loyalty and obedience to Catherine.

MISSION:
To seduce the men the queen had chosen, to obtain information from them, or make them do whatever Catherine ordered.

TECHNIQUES:
The women were trained in espionage and seduction so that they could uncover secrets between kisses.

RULES:
Any woman who disobeyed Catherine or fell pregnant was expelled from the group.

REWARDS:
In return for their services, the queen offered her gratitude, generous rewards and comforts.

METHOD:
At important parties, the female spies were introduced to the guests (ministers, politicians, aristocrats . . .), and they made friends with the powerful gentlemen.

THE SPIES OPERATED AT ALL COURT PARTIES, SEDUCING THE GUESTS WHO HAD BEEN DESIGNATED BY THE QUEEN AS TARGETS.

THE QUEEN LED FRANCE WHEN THE COUNTRY WAS DIVIDED BY THE BITTER CONFLICT BETWEEN THE PROTESTANTS (HUGUENOTS) AND THE CATHOLICS.

THE STAR MISSION

Catherine de Medici used a Flying Squadron member to seduce Antoine de Bourbon. Antoine had been involved in a plot against the young King Francis II, Catherine's son, and the queen decided to hunt her enemy down.

THE BEAUTIFUL YOUNG WOMAN'S MISSION WAS TO ASK ANTOINE DE BOURBON TO SUPPORT CATHERINE IN HER POLITICAL DECISIONS.

For the task, she chose a young girl with sparkling eyes, a perky chest, and ample hips. It was well known that this was the type of woman the king liked.

ANTOINE DE BOURBON,
KING OF NAVARRA

Antoine de Bourbon soon became completely trapped in the spy's web—he fell in love with her on the very first night! He was so keen on the young lady that, at his very first meeting with Catherine, he agreed to her proposal and cleared the ground for the sovereign of France.

CATHERINE HAD WON THE FIRST ROUND.

On another occasion, Catherine de Medici ordered the young woman to tell Antoine de Bourbon that it was impossible for them to be lovers, because he was Protestant and she was Catholic. The following day, the King of Navarre renounced his religion and converted to Catholicism. It caused a great commotion throughout Europe.

DIRTY TRICKS

CATHERINE BECAME THE VICTIM OF A SMEAR CAMPAIGN AND WAS NICKNAMED "THE SERPENT QUEEN."

During the course of her reign, Catherine de Medici became the victim of unfounded smear campaigns that were intended to discredit her. No doubt, it was the price she had to pay for being a woman who was active in politics and who successfully challenged her enemies.

Also, despite her prestigious family name, her Italian origins were frowned upon at the French court.

ART LOVER

Catherine's great interest in astronomy and astrology and her passion for art were also disapproved of by many. The queen amassed an impressive collection of artwork, yet her important role as a patron was never recognized.

Catherine de Medici was a notable ruler of her time despite all this, and she left her mark on both French culture and politics.

GAZETTE DE FRANCE
December 1858

RICHEBOURG

THE 23-INCH SPY

The little man called Richebourg (he was known only by his last name) began his career working as a servant in the court of the Dukes of Orleans. Yet his fate took an unexpected turn with the start of the French Revolution. Richebourg refused to be like the majority of the other little people at the time, who were doomed to work in circuses or to be objects of royal entertainment but became a successful spy of his time.

THE SHORTEST AND CLEVEREST SPY DURING THE FRENCH REVOLUTION.

NAME:
MONSIEUR RICHEBOURG

BORN:
FRANCE, CIRCA 1768

DEATH:
1858 IN PARIS AT THE AGE OF 90

CONFLICT:
THE FRENCH REVOLUTION

PROFILE:
SERVANT TO THE DUKES OF ORLEANS; SPY DURING THE FRENCH REVOLUTION

THE FRENCH REVOLUTION

The French Revolution began in 1789 with the capture of the Bastille and ended in 1799 with the coup led by Napoleon Bonaparte. It was started by France's poorer classes (workers and peasants). They managed to overthrow the monarchy, abolish the aristocracy, and establish the Republic.

THE DUCHESS OF ORLEANS

During one of the most tense phases of the Revolution, when the duchess whom Richebourg was serving realized what was happening, she started to get worried.

She urgently needed to contact her friends in Paris to get the latest updates on the Revolution to find out if she and her court were in danger.

The problem was that the soldiers had cut off the French capital, so the duchess needed someone to infiltrate the city and deliver her letters. When Richebourg found out about the duchess's problem, he volunteered to cross enemy lines and serve as her secret agent.

During the French Revolution, secret agents could be found everywhere. The paranoia was so great that more than 3,000 people were guillotined for working as secret agents against the interests of the Republic between 1794 and 1796.

RICHEBOURG'S STRATEGIES

GETTING INTO PARIS

A woman appeared at the gates of Paris with her baby. The soldiers kindly allowed her to pass through with her little six-month-old girl.

THE BABY WAS THE CUNNING RICHEBOURG IN DISGUISE.

Richebourg had shaved his entire body and beard. He wore baby clothes and sat in a stroller, mostly hidden under a blanket "so he would not get cold."

THE STRATEGY WAS A SUCCESS. RICHEBOURG ENTERED THE CITY AND DELIVERED THE DUCHESS OF ORLEANS' MESSAGES.

Based on his success, Richebourg devised a strategy for other spy missions.

RICHEBOURG IN HIS STROLLER.

INFORMATION FROM THE ENEMY

The female collaborator (the baby's nanny) would leave the baby stroller near the officers or guards from whom she sought information. She simply had to ask them to watch the baby while she ran an errand and the baby slept.

The soldiers were relaxed and chatted calmly in front of the baby, while Richebourg, who had an extraordinary memory, stored all the information in his head. Later, he passed everything he had learned on to the duchess.

NOTABLE MISSIONS

Richebourg and his female collaborators continued to work throughout the entire Revolution. He often crossed enemy lines without raising any suspicion, and barely a few feet from the enemy, he put his hearing and memory to work. He also posed as a lost child to find out secrets at police stations.

The very ingenious spy worked for both sides during the conflict—revolutionaries and supporters of the Old Regime alike. He never took sides and loyally served anyone who sought information and was willing to pay him.

END OF OPERATIONS

Richebourg's ingenious ruse was never uncovered, and he lived out his days as a rich man having completed multiple spy missions.

Le Petit Journal

ADMINISTRATION
61, RUE DE LAFAYETTE, 61

Les manuscrits ne sont pas rendus

On s'abenne sans frais dans tous les bureaux de poste

5 CENT. ILLUSTRATED SUPPLEMENT 5 CENT.

22me Anée ❧❧ Numéro 1.002

WEDNESDAY, MAY 28TH, 1913

ABONNEMENTS

	SIX MOIS	UN AN
SEINE et SEINE-ET-DISE ...	2 FR.	3 FR. 50
DÉPARTEMENTS	2 FR.	4 FR. "
ÉTRANGER	2 50	5 FR. "

ALFRED REDL SPY AND GREAT TRAITOR

NAME:	BORN:	PROFILE:	CONFLICT:	DEATH:
ALFRED REDL	MARCH 14, 1864, IN LEMBERG, THEN AUSTRIA-HUNGARY, NOW UKRAINE	HEAD OF THE AUSTRO-HUNGARIAN MILITARY INTELLIGENCE SERVICE AND RUSSIAN SPY	WORLD WAR I	COMMITTED SUICIDE ON MAY 25, 1913

TRAINING AND CAREER

Alfred Redl was the son of the Austro-Hungarian army officer Franz Redl. Following in his father's footsteps, the young Redl embarked on a career in the army.

After completing his training, Redl was assigned to various bases, where he stood out for his intelligence and ingenuity. In 1900, he was finally promoted to a position in the Vienna Intelligence Service, an office specializing in counterespionage missions.

Alfred Redl worked alongside 20 other officers, transcribing and translating messages with important military information that they would then send in handwritten form to the chief of staff.

THE YOUNG ALFRED STUDIED AT CADET SCHOOL AND AT A WAR SCHOOL WHERE HE GRADUATED WITH HONORS.

REDL SPOKE GERMAN, RUTHENIAN, POLISH, AND RUSSIAN, AND OTHER LANGUAGES. THIS ABILITY WAS KEY IN HIS WORK AND LIFE AS A SPY.

THE GENERAL STAFF

The General Staff is the group in charge of advising and assisting the commander of a military force. It is generally comprised of officers who are highly skilled in strategy, logistics, and military intelligence, and who would send this information in handwritten form to the chief of staff.

RUSSIAN BLACKMAIL

In 1901, the Russian police (the Okhrana) began recruiting spies abroad and sent a headhunter to Vienna, ordering him to capture a high-ranking official harboring an "unspeakable secret."

After nearly three years investigating officers' private lives, the headhunter discovered that a certain captain Redl was involved in a homosexual relationship with a lieutenant.

THE INSTRUCTIONS WERE CLEAR: "EITHER YOU COLLABORATE WITH RUSSIA OR WE REVEAL YOUR SECRET."

Faced with this blackmail that threatened to destroy his promising career and send him to jail, Redl agreed to collaborate with the Okhrana.

PORTRAIT OF ALFRED REDL DURING HIS CADET PHASE, WEARING THE UNIFORM OF THE AUSTRO-HUNGARIAN ARMY.

A NEW LIFE OF LUXURY

Despite having obtained Redl's collaboration by blackmailing him, the Russians paid him very generously for his services.

Redl was soon living a lifestyle that was otherwise reserved only for the aristocracy. He frequented the top restaurants, had a number of cars and horses, and spent huge sums of money on adventures with his lovers.

WITH EVERY DAY THAT WENT BY, HIS LIFE MADE HIM EASIER TO BLACKMAIL.

The story goes that Alfred Redl, driven by greed, also sold the same espionage reports he was sending to the Russians to the French and Italian military.

HE WAS SOON RECEIVING AN EXTRA INCOME OF 50,000 AUSTRIAN KRONEN A YEAR.

MINIATURE CAMERAS AND HIDDEN MICROPHONES

THE DATABASE

At the start of the 20th century, the Austro-Hungarian Empire began to take an interest in the latest technology used in espionage. Miniature cameras and hidden microphones challenged the rudimentary means that spies had been working with up to that point.

THE WOLF HAD BEEN PUT IN CHARGE OF THE HENHOUSE.

HIS INNOVATIVE METHODS WERE NOT USED IN OTHER COUNTRIES UNTIL WORLD WAR II.

And so it was that in 1907, less than a decade before the outbreak of World War I, Captain Redl, who was renowned for his boldness and innovative spirit, was elected as head of the counterintelligence office in the Intelligence Service. Redl's results were celebrated. He spearheaded the use of hidden microphones and other types of modern espionage systems, managing to capture several enemy spies. Redl achieved a number of great successes and rapidly rose up the ranks.

Another of Redl's great innovations was the use of information as a military intelligence weapon. Redl understood the power of secret information and created one of the first databases used to track suspected enemy spies. Redl achieved a number of successes and rapidly rose up the ranks.

IN 1912, REDL WAS NAMED CHIEF OF STAFF OF THE 8TH ARMY CORPS IN PRAGUE.

ARMIES BEGAN TAKING PHOTOS FROM THE SKY USING "SPY PIGEONS."

REMARKABLE MISSIONS

Redl secretly took photos and sent all the Austro-Hungarian army documents that passed through his hands to the Russian army. The full copy of the strategic plan to invade Serbia (Plan III) was a key report that he leaked. The Russians shared it with Serbia, thwarting the invasion of the country in 1914 and culminating in the loss of some 270,000 men serving in the Austro-Hungarian army.

THE TRAITOR ALFRED REDL WAS THE PERSON RESPONSIBLE FOR THE FIASCO THAT WAS THE AUSTRO-HUNGARIAN INVASION OF SERBIA.

Redl also exposed the identities of many Austro-Hungarian spies who were operating inside Russia. Most of them were executed. Investigations show that Redl personally sent Austro-Hungarian spies to Russia in order to then sell their details to the tsar's counterespionage service.

Redl similarly betrayed numerous Russian agents who had established contact with the Austrian intelligence service. He allowed them to be captured, while he was being decorated for his outstanding counterespionage work.

REDL'S LACK OF ETHICS AND SCRUPLES MADE HIM RUSSIA'S MOST IMPORTANT SPY BETWEEN 1903 AND 1913.

END OF OPERATIONS

Redl's life of luxury attracted a lot of attention, prompting an official investigation. Incredibly, as incomprehensible as it may seem, the ingenious spy managed to justify his unusual wealth by claiming it was the result of an inheritance.

On another occasion, Redl was on the verge of being exposed through a leak from a whistleblower, but the investigation of the affair was handed to Redl himself, who naturally brushed it aside.

REDL WAS FINALLY EXPOSED IN 1912.

The story goes that Alfred Redl was eventually exposed and captured thanks to an investigation conducted by the Austro-Hungarian intelligence agency. Today, however, many historians believe that the spy and traitor was actually exposed by a whistleblower and that the Austro-Hungarian intelligence service invented the story of their investigation to avoid being embarrassed by their own incompetence.

DEATH

When it became known that he was a spy, a group of officers secretly met with Alfred Redl in his hotel room. When they explained that his actions had been uncovered, he confessed to some of the facts he was presented with.

REDL CONFESSED THAT, BETWEEN THE YEARS 1910 AND 1911, HE HAD WORKED FOR FOREIGN POWERS WITHOUT ANY ACCOMPLICES.

According to one version of the story, he then asked for a revolver and to be left alone; in another, the Austrian agents gave him the gun without telling him anything because he already knew what this meant and what he had to do.

After the meeting, the officers left the room. That same night, a police officer was sent to the room to certify Redl's death.

REDL HAD TAKEN HIS OWN LIFE BY SHOOTING HIMSELF.

INVESTIGATION

The subsequent police investigation found that Redl's bank accounts had started receiving large sums of unexplained money from 1905, accumulating a total of 116,700 Austrian Kronen in 1913.

This evidence contradicted Redl's confession on the night of his suicide. The General Staff bitterly regretted not having kept the traitor alive for questioning.

At the same time, the General Staff also sought to change the plans and operations that had been leaked by Redl. Yet despite all its efforts, the damage had been done and it was very difficult to improve things on the eve of World War I.

THE ARCHTRAITOR ALFRED REDL WROTE ONE OF THE DARKEST PAGES OF ESPIONAGE HISTORY, CAUSING THE DEATH OF MORE THAN HALF A MILLION OF HIS COMPATRIOTS.

ALFRED REDL WAS ALLEGEDLY PRESSURED INTO COMMITTING SUICIDE BY AUSTRIAN OFFICERS.

CONSPIRACY OF SILENCE

The situation was very serious and threatened to escalate into a national scandal that could call into question the Austrian army's professionalism.

To avoid such a disaster, the senior military officials kept the truth hidden. They sent Emperor Franz Joseph I of Austria a short telegram on the alleged suicide of the chief of staff.

ACCORDING TO THE MESSAGE, REDL HAD COMMITTED SUICIDE "FOR REASONS AS YET UNKNOWN."

Inevitably, the truth eventually came out, and the war ministry had to admit what had really happened only three days after the tragic event.

REDL COMMITTED SUICIDE SO THAT HE WOULD NOT BE TRIED FOR SELLING HIMSELF TO FOREIGN POWERS.

Also in its statement, the war ministry naturally didn't mention that Redl presumably had been forced to commit suicide in a bid to cover up the matter.

FRANZ JOSEPH I OF AUSTRIA WAS KING OF HUNGARY, EMPEROR OF AUSTRIA, AND KING OF BOHEMIA. HIS REIGN LASTED 67 YEARS.

MATA HARI

BEAUTIFUL DANCER IS ARRESTED AND EXECUTED FOR ESPIONAGE

Mata Hari, born Margaretha, had no Asian or Middle Eastern heritage. Her family was Dutch, and her father was a milliner. She had a difficult childhood and adolescence, and once she turned 19, she found a way to escape from everything she had ever known.

Margaretha responded to a newspaper advertisement and agreed to marry Captain Rudolf MacLeod, 20 years her senior. Days after the wedding, the couple moved to Java, Indonesia, where MacLeod was based.

Soon the captain began to abuse Margaretha. She endured the mistreatment until 1903, when she separated from him and moved to Paris to start a new life.

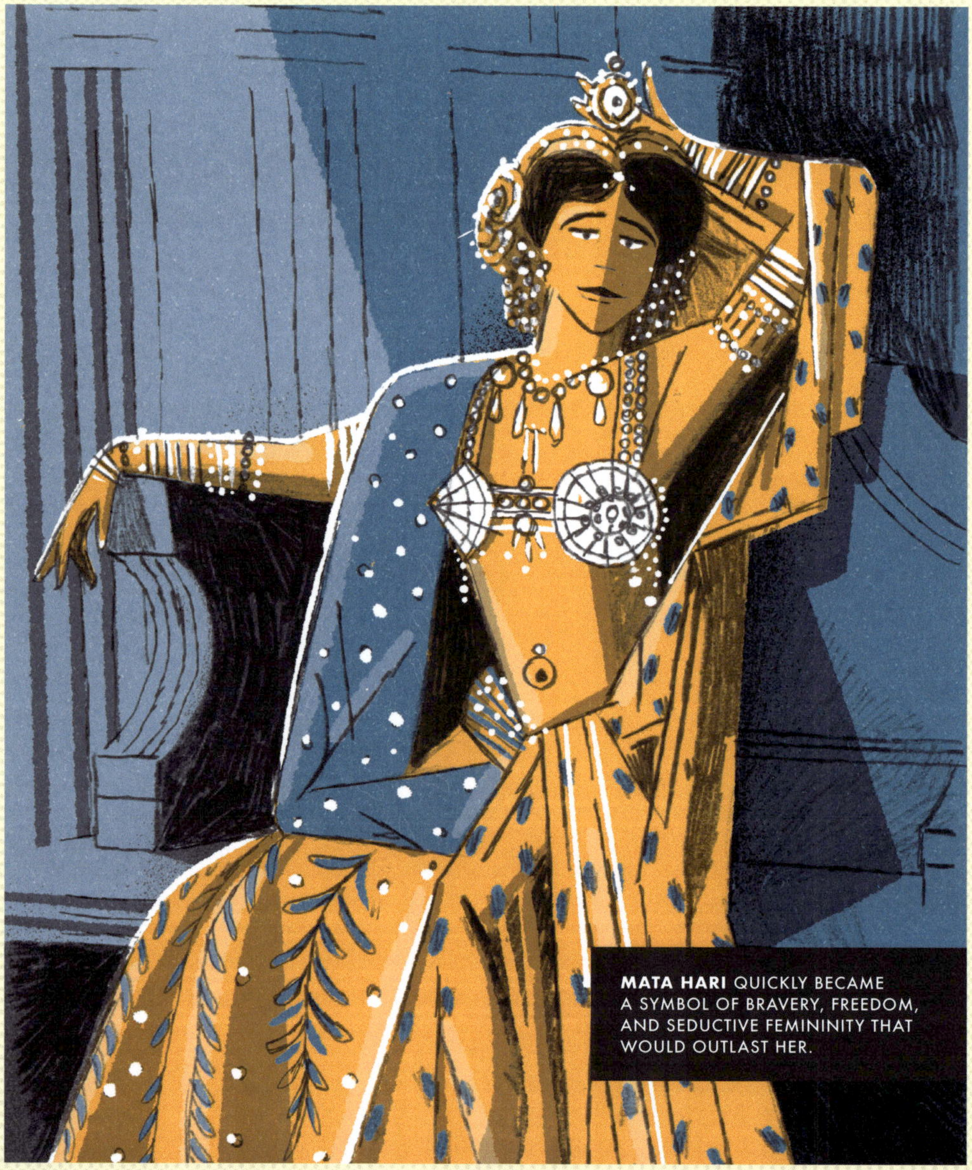

MATA HARI QUICKLY BECAME A SYMBOL OF BRAVERY, FREEDOM, AND SEDUCTIVE FEMININITY THAT WOULD OUTLAST HER.

NAME:

MARGARETHA
GEERTRUIDA ZELLE

ALIAS:

MATA HARI WAS
HER STAGE NAME—
IT MEANS "SUN" IN
MALAY.
HER AGENT CODE
WAS H. 21

BORN:

LEEUWARDEN,
THE NETHERLANDS;
AUGUST 7, 1876

DEATH:

VINCENNES, NEAR
PARIS, FRANCE;
OCTOBER 15, 1917

PROFILE:

DANCER AND
DOUBLE AGENT

THE BIRTH OF MATA HARI: DANCER FROM THE FAR EAST

In 1903, Margaretha arrived in the French capital, where she found work as a model. However, as her income was insufficient, she sought a new career path.

Exotic dancers had become all the rage in Paris at the time, and Margaretha, having learned Oriental dances during her time in Indonesia, soon saw this as an opportunity.

Dressed in stylish robes and sporting stunning dark hair, the brave young woman presented to the world the glorious character that would eventually change the course of her life.

SHE POSED AS "THE JAVANESE PRINCESS MATA HARI TO DELIGHT THE PUBLIC WITH HER DANCES."

MATA HARI IN PARIS IN 1910.

A NEW LIFE

MATA HARI

ENCHANTED HER AUDIENCES WITH HER GRACE AND HER ELEGANT APPEARANCE. THE NEWSPAPERS TALKED OF THE BIRTH OF A NEW STAR.

Mata Hari adopted a unique style to perform traditional Oriental ritual dances, which she claimed she had learned during her childhood in her native land. She won over audiences with her ability to remove several layers of semi transparent veils until all that was left were her breast-plate and jewels.

SHE FILLED THEATERS, AND HIGH SOCIETY AT THE TIME FOUGHT TO SECURE THE BEST FRONT-ROW SEATS AT HER SHOWS.

RELATIONS WITH HIGH SOCIETY

Mata Hari was an applauded performer at theaters all over Europe. Her success enabled her to establish secret relationships with influential figures in society.

Men were fascinated by her charms, sophistication, and, of course, her defiant speeches. Mata Hari conquered the stages of the top theaters just as easily as she seduced the richest and most powerful men in the world.

Wilhelm, crown prince of Germany, was one of her most besotted lovers. Mata Hari believed her relationship with the heir to the German throne would be her chance to be part of the royal family, but all those plans were destroyed by the outbreak of World War I. The prince shifted his focus to military matters and cut ties with the exotic dancer.

THE FRENCH SECRET SERVICE SOON REALIZED HER RELATIONS COULD MAKE HER A VERY USEFUL SPY.

MATA HARI IN 1905, PERFORMING ONE OF HER "BRAHMANIC DANCES" IN THE LIBRARY OF THE GUIMET MUSEUM IN PARIS.

WORLD WAR I

World War I began in Europe in 1914 and lasted until 1918. It was fought between two enemy sides: the Central Powers (Germany, Austria-Hungary, and later the Ottoman Empire, and Bulgaria) and the Triple Entente—a coalition of Great Britain, France, and Russia. Italy joined the alliance in 1915, and the USA in 1917. In the same year, Russia withdrew after the Revolution.

During the war, Mata Hari managed to establish relations with several high-ranking soldiers from all over Europe. Her Dutch passport (the Netherlands being a neutral country) enabled her to travel freely throughout the continent.

MATA HARI BECAME THE SECRET LOVER OF MILITARY LEADERS ON BOTH SIDES OF THE CONFLICT DURING WORLD WAR I.

MATA HARI AND CAPTAIN VADIM MASLOV.

THE GREAT LOVE OF HER LIFE

The great love of her life was a young Russian officer named Vadim Maslov, who, within months of meeting her, lost an eye in the bloody battles of 1916.

Mata Hari asked the French authorities for permission to visit Maslov in the field hospital, but the French intelligence service quickly intervened and imposed a condition.

MATA HARI COULD VISIT VADIM MASLOV IF SHE AGREED TO COLLABORATE AS A SPY.

DOUBLE AGENT

ONE YEAR EARLIER, MATA HARI HAD STARTED WORKING FOR THE GERMANS AS AGENT H. 21.

What the French didn't know was that Mata Hari had already been working for the Germans as a secret agent since 1915.

The story goes that a year after the war began, Mata Hari found herself in the Netherlands. The conflict made it impossible for the young woman to return to Paris, where she was working at a distinguished salon. It was then that the German consul in Amsterdam (Karl Kroemer) arranged for her to visit Paris if she agreed to provide him with information from the Allies.

The Germans knew Mata Hari could be an important source of information. Her Parisian salon attracted highly influential people and prominent military figures from the French armed forces.

BOTH SIDES WANTED MATA HARI TO USE HER POWERS OF SEDUCTION TO OBTAIN INFORMATION FROM THE MEN IN CONTROL.

MISSIONS

She is believed to have performed her most important espionage operation when she returned to Paris and resumed her work at the salon. The clientele included a number of officers from the Allied Forces. Mata Hari used her charms to obtain information that she then sent to Germany.

Legend has it that the seductive courtesan sourced valuable information from French and British officers—information that even the best German intelligence agents would otherwise never have been able to access.

But Mata Hari claimed that the information she offered to the Germans was merely gossip relating to the private lives of various officers or politicians, and was of little military value.

WHILE SHE MAY NOT HAVE BEEN EFFECTIVE AS A SPY, HER LEGEND MADE HER FAMOUS IN SPY CIRCLES.

END OF OPERATION: THE UNMASKING

THE MESSAGE

In January 1917, the French intelligence service intercepted a coded message that has been transmitted from Berlin.

In this message, German officer Arnold von Kalle offered his superiors key information on secret agent H. 21 (including addresses, bank details, and even her handmaid's name), thus exposing Mata Hari's hideaways and identity.

MATA HARI WAS ARRESTED IN HER PARIS HOTEL ROOM A FEW WEEKS LATER.

INTERROGATIONS

Mata Hari was questioned over a period of several weeks.

According to reports, she was first transferred to London, where the British secret service interrogated her—without achieving any results. She was then transferred to France via Spain.

The dancer had no problem acknowledging her intimate relations with officers on both sides, but she always insisted on her loyalty to the Allies. She claimed that she never provided the Germans with information that could put French troops at risk.

MATA HARI ON THE DAY OF HER ARREST, FEBRUARY 13, 1917.

TRIAL

Mata Hari was quickly abandoned by everyone. None of her friends, acquaintances, or lovers visited her in prison.

During her trial, she was accused of being the German spy responsible for the deaths of some 50,000 French soldiers. In the end, despite a lack of solid evidence against her, she was sentenced to death.

IF SOLDIERS DIED, IT WAS NOT BECAUSE OF INCOMPETENCE OF SENIOR OFFICIALS. IT WAS BECAUSE OF THE TREASON COMMITTED BY AN IMMORAL FOREIGN DIVORCÉE.

"I AM PROUD OF MY PAST AND I WAS NEVER A SPY, BUT I WAS MATA HARI!"

THE TRIAL OF MATA HARI.

MATA HARI'S SENTENCE WAS PRESENTED AS A VICTORY OF THE FRENCH SECURITY SERVICE.

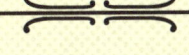

MATA HARI, WAITING TO BE EXECUTED BY THE FIRING SQUAD.

EXECUTION

INVESTIGATION

The famous dancer was executed by a firing squad comprised of 12 French soldiers, just before daybreak on October 15, 1917. She was 41 years old.

Legend has it that Mata Hari refused to be blindfolded. The star performer fell slowly to the ground, her head held upright, without changing her facial expression.

MATA HARI DIED AS ELEGANTLY AS SHE HAD LIVED.

A dossier published by the German government in 1930 confirmed that the reports on Mata Hari had not been of any military use.

Investigations also found that as revenge, the Germans sent the message in a code that had already been deciphered by the French—in a bid to expose Mata Hari's identity and thus force her execution.

Ultimately, Mata Hari was the victim of an unfair, sexist system. But despite her sad end, she became a symbol of bravery, freedom, and femininity. Her story inspired women from all over the world to follow their dreams and not be afraid of challenging society's standard expectations.

THE EVIDENCE PRESENTED WAS DUBIOUS OR INDEED EVEN FABRICATED, AND IT IS BELIEVED THAT MATA HARI WAS THE SCAPEGOAT OF A COUNTRY THAT WAS LOSING THE WAR.

Ace of Spies is executed by the secret police of the Soviet Union.

Daily Mail.

WORLD'S LARGEST NET DAILY SALE.

LONDON.   MANCHESTER.   PARIS.   THURSDAY, 26 NOVEMBER 1925   ONE PENNY.   POSTAGE { IN U. K. 1d
ABROAD 1 ¼d.

THIRD EDITION

**Royal Wedding
Picture Number**

SIDNEY REILLY

THE LEGENDARY AGENT EXECUTED BY STALIN

"THE ACE OF SPIES" FALLS INTO THE SOVIET DICTATOR'S TRAP NEAR MOSCOW.

A LOVER OF BEAUTIFUL WOMEN AND WITH A PENCHANT FOR LUXURY, HE MAY HAVE BEEN THE INSPIRATION FOR JAMES BOND.

HIS TRUE IDENTITY

NAME:
HIS REAL NAME IS NOT KNOWN. IT MAY HAVE BEEN SIGMUND (SHLOMO) ROSENBLUM

ALIAS:
SIDNEY GEORGE REILLY, NICKNAMED "THE ACE OF SPIES"

BORN:
MARCH 24, 1874, IN ODESSA (RUSSIA, TODAY'S UKRAINE)

DEATH:
EXECUTED NEAR MOSCOW ON NOVEMBER 5, 1925

PROFILE:
ENTREPRENEUR AND SECRET AGENT, LOVER OF LUXURY

CONFLICT:
THE RUSSIAN REVOLUTION

Sidney Reilly was born in the city of Odessa in the former Russian Empire (present-day Ukraine). It is believed that his father was a doctor and his mother a member of the Russian aristocracy. He may have been the only child of Pauline and Gregory Rosenblum, a wealthy Jewish couple, but his origins are very unclear.

It is said that the ace of spies lived a lavish lifestyle, filled with adventures and visits to exotic locations, always surrounded by beautiful women, although many of the stories about Reilly were invented by Reilly himself.

Calling himself Rosenblum, he worked as an informer for the Russian tsar's police. When the tsarist regime was toppled, he opposed the Bolsheviks who had come to power.

THE TSARIST REGIME

The Russian Empire lasted from the 18th century until the Russian Revolution in 1917, when the tsar was forced to abdicate. Until then, he controlled most of the country's power and wealth. The Bolshevik (communist) victory marked the end of the Russian Empire.

PHOTOGRAPH OF REILLY IN A COUNTERFEIT PASSPORT.

HIS TRUE IDENTITY REMAINS A MYSTERY TO THIS DAY AND HYPOTHESES ABOUND—SUCH AS PASSPORT PICTURES.

A NEW LIFE IN BRAZIL

In 1896, the mysterious man moved to Brazil, where he worked as a cook and port laborer and also found jobs in the countryside.

It was in Brazil that he saved one of his bosses, Charles Fothergill, from an assassination attempt. According to eyewitnesses, the daring Reilly grabbed a gun and killed Fothergill's attackers with outstanding marksmanship.

To show his gratitude, his boss rewarded him with 1,500 pounds, a ticket to London, and a British passport that identified him as Sidney Rosenblum.

WHILE A MAN OF IMPECCABLE MANNERS AND TASTE, HE DID NOT HAVE MANY SCRUPLES.

THERE, DESPITE HIS RUSSIAN BLOOD, HE MINGLED WITH THE EXCLUSIVE BRITISH JET SET.

LONDON

Once in the British capital, the adventurer founded a medicine company known as Ozone Preparations. Legend has it that to establish this company, he robbed two anarchists on a train traveling from Paris to Fontainebleau. With his Polish accomplice, Yan Voitek, he murdered them in cold blood and stole the money that had been intended to finance revolutionary acts.

Sidney managed to become part of the British jet set and the same year, married Margaret Callaghan Thomas, the young millionaire widow of the Reverend Hugh Thomas, who had changed his will in favor of his wife only a week before dying, supposedly, of the flu.

SIDNEY MAY WELL HAVE POISONED THE REVEREND HUGH THOMAS IN ORDER TO MARRY HIS WEALTHY WIDOW.

SCOTLAND YARD

In 1899, Sidney Reilly met William Melville, a bigwig at Scotland Yard (London's police force). Melville then created a new identity for Sidney and hired him as a spy for the British Empire.

AND SO ROSENBLUM BECAME SIDNEY REILLY.

This first assumed identity marked the start of his legendary series of feats.

REMARKABLE MISSIONS

Sidney Reilly secured a position in the Foreign Section of the British Secret Service Bureau, the precursor to the modern-day Intelligence Service (better known as MI6).

During World War I, he lived in New York, where he became a millionaire selling ammunition to both Germany and Russia while collaborating with the British secret service.

Among many other missions, Reilly is believed to have stolen the maps of Port Arthur (which facilitated a Japanese attack on the Russians in 1904), enabled a British oil company to be purchased in the Persian Gulf (Persian Oil Company), and helped the resistance against the Bolsheviks in Russia.

THE BOLSHEVIK REVOLUTION

Starvation and outrage were the driving forces that prompted the Russian people to stand up to Tsar Nicholas II. The people's uprising against the tsar was led by Vladimir Ilyich Ulyanov, better known as Lenin. The Bolsheviks took power, promising "peace, bread, and land," and following a violent revolution, they established a communist government and created the Soviet Union (1922).

ONE SOLE OBSESSION

HIS PRIMARY INTENT WAS ALWAYS TO ASSASSINATE LENIN.

Throughout his life, Reilly used different identities, practiced multiple professions, and worked for the highest bidder. But he always had one clear objective that took priority over everything else.

"BOLSHEVISM HAD A BAPTISM OF FIRE... ITS LEADERS WERE CRIMINALS AND MURDERERS," THE FAMOUS SPY IS REPORTED TO HAVE SAID.

In 1918, he traveled to Russia, where he planned to assassinate Lenin, the man he so despised. But the mission failed, and he had to escape.

SOME OF HIS LOVERS OFFERED HIM SHELTER, AND SO THE CASANOVA AVOIDED CAPTURE AND EXECUTION BY THE SOVIET AUTHORITIES.

LENIN, THE UNDISPUTED LEADER OF THE BOLSHEVIK REVOLUTION.

ONE FINAL MARRIAGE

Reilly married several times, but he never bothered to get divorced. During a visit to Berlin in December 1922, he met a charming actress by the name of Pepita Bobadilla.

She was an attractive young blond who claimed, falsely, to be South American. Her real name was Nelly Burton, and she had recently risen to fame, thanks to her career as a music hall entertainer and dancer.

On May 18, 1923, the couple married at Covent Garden, in central London. Since Reilly was still married at the time, he ended up with two wives. Their union lasted barely 30 months, before the spy disappeared in Russia.

SIDNEY REILLY ON THE DAY OF HIS WEDDING TO THE ACTRESS PEPITA BOBADILLA IN 1923.

OPERATION TRUST
A COMMUNIST PLOT

In September 1925, Reilly returned to the Soviet Union to meet with the members of a new anticommunist organization. However, the supposed meeting ended up being part of "Operation Trust," a trap orchestrated by the Soviet dictator Stalin.

The ploy devised by Stalin's counterintelligence service revolved around promoting a fake anti-Bolshevik movement to ensnare members of the anticommunist resistance and arrest them.

SIDNEY REILLY, THE SPY WHO SOUGHT TO ASSASSINATE LENIN, FELL INTO STALIN'S TRAP.

THE END

Despite his great experience and cunning, Reilly was caught up in the trap along with the other members, and he was executed in a forest near Moscow in November 1925. The order for his execution was signed by Joseph Stalin.

DESPITE THE RISKY NATURE OF HIS WORK AS A SPY, IT WAS ULTIMATELY HIS INVOLVEMENT IN THE ANTICOMMUNIST RESISTANCE THAT KILLED REILLY.

EL NACIONAL

AL SERVICIO DE LA COLECTIVIDAD

2ª Sección

NUM. 4,079—2a. EPOCA
AÑO XIL—TOMO XVII

MÉXICO, D. F., THURSDAY, AUGUST 22, 1940

Departamento Comercial
RAUL ORTEGA

REGISTRADO COMO ARTÍCULO DE 1a. EN LA ADMON. DE CORREOS EL 18 DE FEB. DE 1820

RAMÓN MERCADER

THE SECRET AGENT WHO ASSASSINATED TROTSKY

Ramón Mercader was the second son of a middle-class Barcelona family. Pablo Mercader, his father, was a businessman and politically conservative, and Caridad del Río, his mother, a Cuban revolutionary. The marriage soon failed, and del Rio dedicated her life to revolution.

MERCADER IN A POLICE MUG SHOT
IN 1935. HE WAS ARRESTED AND IMPRISONED FOR DISTRIBUTING COMMUNIST PROPAGANDA.

NAME:	ALIASES:	BORN:	DEATH:	PROFILE:	CONFLICT:
JAIME RAMÓN MERCADER DEL RIO	JACQUES MORNARD; RAMÓN IVANOVITCH LÓPEZ; FRANK JACKSON	FEBRUARY 7, 1913, IN BARCELONA, SPAIN	OCTOBER 18, 1978, IN HAVANA, CUBA	COMMUNIST AND SOVIET SECRET AGENT	SPANISH CIVIL WAR AND THE FIGHT FOR LENIN'S SUCCESSOR

COMMUNIST, LIKE HIS MOTHER

In 1931, the 18-year-old Mercader was an attractive, bright young man who, following in his mother's footsteps, devoted his life to communism.

He and his comrades attended meetings, demonstrations, and communist campaigns. When the Spanish Civil War broke out, he also took up arms and fought on the front for the republican movement alongside his mother.

After a year, however, both he and his mother gave up their fight in the Spanish war, and del Rio convinced her son to join the Soviet secret service in a challenging mission:

TO ASSASSINATE LEON TROTSKY.

TROTSKY IN THE STUDY OF THE HOUSE WHERE HE WAS ASSASSINATED.

LEON TROTSKY

Leon Trotsky was key in the success of the Russian Revolution against the tsarist regime. But after Lenin's death, Trotsky became one of the candidates for ruling the Soviet Union in a face-off against Stalin. Relentlessly persecuted by Stalin, Trotsky was forced to flee the country. He lived in exile in Mexico, where he mixed with intellectuals and artists who included the likes of Diego Rivera and Frida Kahlo.

Despite being far from Russia, Trotsky never ceased to criticize Stalin, prompting the Soviet leader to decide to have him assassinated.

PLANNING

MERCADER AND AGELOFF HAD A PASSIONATE ROMANCE IN PARIS, WHICH CONTINUED VIA LETTERS WHEN SHE RETURNED TO NEW YORK.

1. TRAINING

In 1937, Mercader received Soviet training in a secret location. He then had his base in Paris, where he was reunited with his mother.

2. INFILTRATION

In Paris, Mercader infiltrated French Trotskyist circles using a fake identity. Mercader went by the name of Jacques Mornard and managed to convince everyone that he was a Belgian militant and the son of a diplomat. Mercader used his great knowledge and language proficiency to adopt false identities.

3. SEDUCING SYLVIA AGELOFF

The young imposter was in his element among the Trotskyists. Then, just before the Fourth International was established, Trotsky's secretary and confidante, Sylvia Ageloff arrived in Paris. Mercader was a ladies' man and turned on the charm to win her heart, and the naïve Sylvia Ageloff fell head over heels into the trap set by the Soviet agent.

THE YOUNG SECRETARY, **SYLVIA AGELOFF.**

OPERATION "DUCK"

JOSEF STALIN INITIATES OPERATION "DUCK."

After several years of planning, Josef Stalin decided it was time to assassinate Leon Trotsky, and he promptly set about activating the agents who had been recruited and trained specifically for the mission.

Stalin sent Leonid Aleksandrovich Eitingon, the Soviet agent in charge of training and assisting Mercader and his mother in the final, lethal attack to Paris.

Mother and son continued their training in New York, and despite the fact that Stalin ordered them to return to Europe at the outbreak of World War II, Mercader decided to go directly to Mexico, accompanied by Sylvia Ageloff.

The first assassination attempt came in the early hours of May 24, when a group of armed men entered Trotsky's house with the help of one of his bodyguards, a double agent. The operation was a failure—they didn't even manage to injure the target. Stalin grew impatient and implemented the backup plan, spearheaded by Mercader.

FIRST DIRECT CONTACT WITH TROTSKY

Mercader had spent several months in Mexico posing as Sylvia Ageloff's boyfriend. Over time, he became a familiar face to Trotsky's entourage, and soon after the first failed assassination attempt, he managed to get to know Trotsky personally.

MERCADER HAD NO TROUBLE FORGING A RELATIONSHIP WITH THE EXILED LEADER.

LETHAL ATTACK

On the sunny morning of August 20, 1940, Mercader headed to Trotsky's office on the pretext of asking him to review an article he had written.

Trotsky was on his own there, and as he went over to the window to read the documents, he was struck on the head with an ice axe. He managed to grab hold of Mercader to stop him and let out a wail of agony that alerted his guards. del Rio and Eitingon were waiting near the property but fled when they realized the assassin wasn't coming back.

THE ASSASSIN'S **WEAPON.**

TROTSKY DID NOT DIE INSTANTLY. HE SUFFERED FOR 12 HOURS BEFORE PASSING AWAY.

SYLVIA AGELOFF TRIED TO COMMIT SUICIDE WHEN SHE FOUND OUT THAT MERCADER WANTED TO KILL TROTSKY.

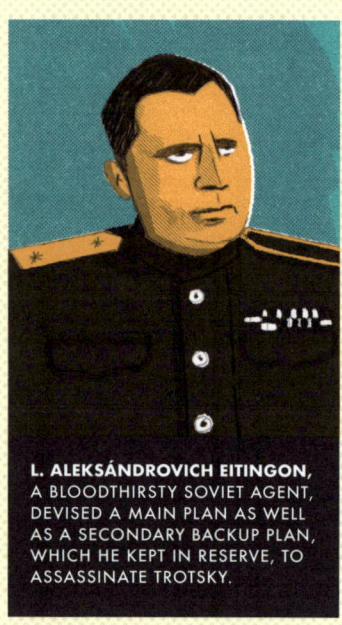

L. ALEKSÁNDROVICH EITINGON, A BLOODTHIRSTY SOVIET AGENT, DEVISED A MAIN PLAN AS WELL AS A SECONDARY BACKUP PLAN, WHICH HE KEPT IN RESERVE, TO ASSASSINATE TROTSKY.

TROTSKY'S PROPERTY IN MEXICO CITY.

ARREST

RAMÓN MERCADER WAS SENTENCED TO 20 YEARS IN PRISON FOR THE ASSASSINATION.

RAMÓN MERCADER DURING HIS ARREST AFTER TROTSKY'S ASSASSINATION.

Mercader was detained by Trotsky's bodyguards and the Mexican authorities. The Soviet agent identified himself as Jacques Mornard, claiming he had personal issues with Trotsky. He never revealed the real plot behind the crime he had committed.

HIS MOTHER AND EITINGON'S ESCAPE

Del Rio and Eitingon were waiting for Mercader in the vicinity of Trotsky's home, but they fled when they saw the police cars arrive. Eitingon immediately left the country, and del Rio followed soon after. On June 17, 1941, the NKVD (senior Soviet officials) organized a huge reception and awarded the Order of Lenin to the woman.

DEL RIO ARRIVED IN MOSCOW AFTER HIRING AN ATTORNEY FOR HER SON.

OPERATION "GNOME"

Stalin simultaneously initiated Operation "Gnome" to free Mercader from prison. Various escape plans were assessed that could be enacted by Soviet agents, Mexican communists, and Spanish communists exiled in the country.

Nevertheless, the Mexican authorities clamped down on Mercader's jail term, and he had to serve the full sentence.

THE OPERATIONS FELL FLAT WHEN HIS MOTHER APPEARED ON THE SCENE.

AFTER A 20-YEAR SENTENCE

On May 6, 1960, Ramón Mercader finished his sentence and traveled to Moscow, where he was made a Hero of the Soviet Union by being awarded the Order of Lenin and the Gold Star medal, the Soviet Union's highest honor. He was also given a prestigious position within the KGB.

DEATH

Mercader spent his final years between Moscow and Cuba, where he became Fidel Castro's adviser.

He finally died of cancer in Cuba in 1978. A dark legend has it that the KGB poisoned him with a polonium laced watch that was presented to him for his services.

His body was secretly transported to Moscow and buried in a cemetery for the heroes of the Soviet Union.

LA VANGUARDIA

BARCELONA
Año LVL – Número 23.019

DIARIO AL SERVICIO DE LA DEMOCRACIA
Oficinas: Pelayo, 28 – Telefono 1413

15 céntimos
Thursday, June 7, 1945

THE DOUBLE AGENT WHO OUTWITTED HITLER

JOAN PUJOL, DISTINGUISHED BY HIS CUNNING, HIS INTERPRETING SKILLS, AND HIS NON-VIOLENT APPROACH.

THE SPY FACILITATED THE ALLIES' SUCCESSFUL LANDINGS IN NORMANDY.

JOAN PUJOL

NAME:	ALIAS:	BORN:	PROFILE:	CONFLICT:	DEATH:
JOAN PUJOL GARCÍA	GARBO (BRITISH ALIAS), ARABEL (GERMAN ALIAS)	1912, IN BARCELONA	DOUBLE AGENT, CONSIDERED ONE OF THE MOST EFFECTIVE SPIES OF WORLD WAR II	WORLD WAR II	1988, IN CARACAS, VENEZUELA

AN OPPONENT OF NAZISM

BARRICADES AGAINST THE FRANCOIST TROOPS IN BARCELONA ON JULY 19, 1936.

Joan Pujol was born to a wealthy family in Barcelona in 1912. But his calm, quiet life suddenly changed completely when civil war broke out in Spain in the summer of 1936.

FRANCO'S MILITARY REBELLION IN SPAIN SPARKED A WAR IN WHICH PUJOL LOST FAMILY AND FRIENDS.

The tragedies brought about by this conflict turned Pujol against Europe's authoritarian governments, and he decided to become involved in the fight against Adolf Hitler's Nazi Germany, a. k. a. the Third Reich.

THE SPANISH CIVIL WAR

Between 1936 and 1939, the people of Spain found themselves split into two camps: the republicans and the nationalists. The former advocated a secular, modern, and progressive Spain, while the latter aspired to a traditional and conservative Spain founded on the church and armed forces. The war had devastating consequences for the country, and the victory by the military rebels culminated in Francisco Franco's dictatorship.

REJECTED BY THE ALLIES

In 1940, with World War II in full swing, Joan Pujol decided to travel to Spanish capital of Madrid and then head to the British embassy.

The United Kingdom was the main enemy of the National Socialist regime in Germany at the time, and the young man offered his services to work as a secret agent for the Allied forces. The British, however, rejected his offer.

Pujol was not to be deterred, though. On the contrary, he decided to approach the Germans and talk them into believing that he was a British government spy. This time, his improvised strategy worked, and he was recruited by Nazi officer Karl Erich Kühlenthal.

HE BECAME A SECRET AGENT FOR THE NATIONAL SOCIALIST REGIME.

A NAZI SPY

Pujol performed his initial secret operations out of Lisbon, even though he told the Germans he was in the United Kingdom. He was very skilled at drawing up elaborate false reports on merchant-boat routes.

HE MANAGED TO CONVINCE THE GERMANS THAT HIS INFORMATION WAS VERY VALUABLE.

He used information found in the international media to add credibility to his fabrications. He also pretended to travel all over the country, sending records of his expenses to Germany based on prices he copied from British railway guides.

DOUBLE AGENT

After a few months of pretending to collaborate with the Germans, Pujol once again offered his services to the British, and this time, he was accepted.

What he didn't know was that the British intelligence service had been monitoring his activities all along and was well aware of his collaboration with the Germans.

HE WAS AGENT "GARBO" TO THE ALLIES AND "ARABEL" TO THE NAZIS.

A FAKE SPY NETWORK

In the spring of 1942, while he was based in the United Kingdom, Pujol convinced the Germans that he was recruiting agents to create a new network of spies who would swear loyalty to Hitler and the Third Reich.

Of course, none of those individuals actually existed. He fabricated detailed reports on all the fake agents, who included some very powerful people.

GARBO CREATED 22 CHARACTERS FOR HIS FICTITIOUS NETWORK.

A JIGSAW PUZZLE

Inventing reports from each agent without falling into contradictions was very difficult. Sometimes, Pujol had to justify to the Germans why one of his fictitious agents had not leaked information that, due to his supposed position, he should have known.

THE NAZIS PAID HIM LARGE SUMS OF MONEY FOR THE IMAGINARY SPY RING.

To make his reports look more convincing, Garbo included authentic reports of events and data but delayed their submission to minimize the impact. He used pre-dated postage stamps on reports that he sent when the information no longer endangered the Allied troops.

THE GERMAN GOVERNMENT BOUGHT REPORTS ON SECRET AGENTS WHO DID NOT EXIST.

REMARKABLE MISSIONS

OPERATION FORTITUDE

PUJOL CLAIMED THE NORMANDY LANDINGS WERE A DISTRACTION TO WARD OFF HITLER'S TROOPS.

Pujol's greatest feat of disinformation was Operation Fortitude. Agent Garbo managed to convince Hitler that the Allied troops' landings in Europe were going to take place via the Strait of Dover, when they were actually going to be happening along the Normandy beaches.

His power of persuasion and the confidence Hitler had in him meant that even when the first troops began to arrive in Normandy, the Führer believed that they were part of a distraction tactic.

The Nazis kept their troops at the wrong location, more than 125 miles away, and by the time they realized that they had been tricked, it was too late. The Allies' D-Day landings had been a major success.

THE D-DAY LANDINGS IN NORMANDY

The military operation known as D-Day saw the Allied troops land by both sea and air to gain a strategic position, a support base on the beaches of the northern French coast in Normandy, before continuing their advance toward the interior of the continent.

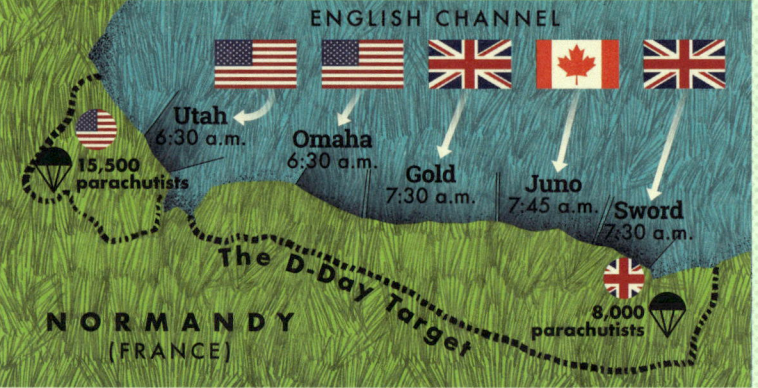

ENGLISH CHANNEL

15,500 parachutists

Utah 6:30 a.m.

Omaha 6:30 a.m.

Gold 7:30 a.m.

Juno 7:45 a.m.

Sword 7:30 a.m.

The D-Day Target

8,000 parachutists

NORMANDY (FRANCE)

AMERICAN TROOPS APPROACHING OMAHA BEACH TO LAND IN NORMANDY ON JUNE 6, 1944.

PUJOL'S ABILITY OF DECEIVE HITLER WAS ONE OF THE KEY MOMENTS OF WORLD WAR II.

PUJOL WAS PROUD TO HAVE PARTICIPATED IN TWO WARS WITHOUT KILLING ANYONE HIMSELF OR FIRING A SINGLE SHOT.

The BBC, the British broadcaster, also played an important role in the war. Pujol used its broadcasts to send hidden messages to the French Resistance and Allied spies. These messages, coupled with the fake information supplied by Garbo, ended up being critical to the Allies' victory in World War II.

THIS FAMOUS POEM BY PAUL VERLAINE:

THE LONG SOBS OF THE VIOLINS OF AUTUMN WOUND MY HEART WITH A MONOTONOUS LANGUOR

WAS USED TO ALERT THE FRENCH RESISTANCE THAT THE ANTICIPATED NORMANDY LANDINGS WOULD BE TAKING PLACE THE FOLLOWING DAY.

THE SPY RETIRES

Pujol stopped working as a secret agent once the war was over. The double agent ceased his intelligence missions and moved to Venezuela with his family. He died in Caracas in 1988.

Pujol is remembered as one of the most outstanding spies of World War II.

INVESTIGATION

Pujol was never actually accused of any crime, and he was held in equally high esteem by both the Germans and the Allied forces for his intelligence work and bravery.

PUJOL IS THE ONLY PERSON INVOLVED IN WORLD WAR II TO HAVE BEEN DECORATED BY BOTH SIDES.

FRIDAY, JUNE 8, 1945

Evening Standard

LONG JOHN

FINAL NIGHT EXTRA ●

37,476 DIM-OUT 6.21 pro 1a 7.9 am MOON flying 1.53 pm. Sets 19 pm ONE PENNY

THE NAZIS' MOST WANTED SPY WAS A WOMAN

NANCY WAKE

"THE WHITE MOUSE"

Restless and adventurous, Nancy Wake ran away from home and the poverty of her Sydney childhood at the age of 16. She soon left Australia and traveled to New York, using the modest inheritance left to her by an aunt.

From the USA, Wake moved on to Europe, and after funding her own journalism studies in London, she moved to Paris and began to work as a press correspondent. The young globetrotter did not yet know that she was going to be a spy.

WAKE FREELY AND BRAVELY TRAVELED THE WORLD FOLLOWING HER DREAMS.

NANCY WAKE WOULD GO ON TO HAVE A DECORATED LIFE OF ADVENTURE.

NAME:	ALIAS:	BORN:	PROFILE:	CONFLICT:	DEATH:
NANCY GRACE AUGUSTA WAKE	"THE WHITE MOUSE"	AUGUST 30, 1912, IN WELLINGTON, NEW ZEALAND	NURSE AND JOURNALIST	WORLD WAR II	AUGUST 7, 2011, AT THE AGE OF 98

BERLIN CORRESPONDENT

Although Wake lived in Paris, her work as a correspondent often took her to other countries. While based in Berlin, she experienced Adolf Hitler's rise to power firsthand. In Vienna, she interviewed the Führer and witnessed the first round of persecutions by the Nazis.

After her stints in Germany and Austria, Wake was horrified at the way the Jewish people were being treated and decided to fight against Hitler.

WAKE MET HENRI FIOCCA, HER FUTURE HUSBAND, UPON HER RETURN TO PARIS.

OCCUPATION OF FRANCE

Back in Paris, the young journalist fell in love with Henri E. Fiocca, a wealthy French businessman. The couple married in 1939 and moved to Marseille on the Mediterranean coast. This is where they lived when Nazi Germany invaded France in 1940.

WAKE LOVED HER HUSBAND, BUT SHE ALSO LOVED FRANCE, AND THE WAR PUT HER IN A DIFFICULT POSITION.

RESISTANCE LEADER

SHE ORGANIZED AN ESCAPE ROUTE ACROSS THE PYRENEES.

The network eventually included several thousand soldiers, who took charge of maintaining the escape route, provided information to the Allies, committed acts of sabotage, and carried out direct attacks.

Far from turning a blind eye to what was happening, Wake and Fiocca decided to get involved in the fight against the Third Reich, and the pair joined the French Resistance.

Wake's participation in the Resistance movement against the Nazi occupation was key.

BEING A WOMAN MADE HER LESS SUSPICIOUS TO THE GERMANS.

Wake was stylish, cultured, and rich, and the Nazis did not suspect her. She began to collaborate as a messenger, and later organized an escape network that enabled persecuted peoples (Jews, Allied soldiers and others) to leave France.

THE MAQUIS

The Resistance groups operating in occupied France hid in remote and mountainous areas to avoid capture. They committed acts of sabotage, attacked enemy forces, and provided help and shelter to Allies and persecuted people.

ONE OF THE ROUTES USED TO ESCAPE FROM FRANCE.

NAZIS PERPLEXED

The Gestapo tried to dismantle the Resistance's escape network. They managed to capture the British army captain Ian Garrow, Wake's contact operating out of London, who was coordinating the refugees' arrival.

Garrow was tortured to reveal the identity of his local collaborator in France, but he did not betray Wake.

GARROW DID NOT CONFESS TO COLLABORATING WITH WAKE.

THE GESTAPO

The Gestapo was the secret state police of the Third Reich. Its task was to investigate, quash, persecute, and deport anyone opposing the Nazi regime. The Gestapo used arrest, torture, and assassination as means of eliminating its enemies and keeping control of the state.

IAN GARROW, BRITISH ARMY CAPTAIN.

THE LEGEND OF "THE WHITE MOUSE"

WAFFEN-SS

EINTRITT NACH VOLLENDETEM 17. LEBENSJAHR

THE WAFFEN-SS WERE THE ELITE COMBAT FORCES OF GERMANY'S NAZI PARTY.

THE GESTAPO NICKNAMED WAKE "THE WHITE MOUSE" BECAUSE SHE WAS SO ELUSIVE.

The mysterious person in charge of the escape network became a real obsession and nightmare for the Gestapo, who were never able to uncover their true identity.

Wake, who was leading the Resistance in the south of France, always managed to outwit the Gestapo and was never discovered by the Germans.

THE NAZIS PUT A HEFTY BOUNTY OF FIVE MILLION FRANCS ON HER HEAD.

DETAINED

An inspection conducted in the French city of Toulouse led to the Nazis arresting Wake, but after a few days of questioning, the occupiers let her go. She had managed to convince them that she was merely on a business trip.

THEY NEVER DISCOVERED THAT THE ENIGMATIC "WHITE MOUSE" WAS A WOMAN.

The young journalist's luck ran out in October 1943, however, when an informer leaked her address, and the Germans were able to identify the home of Nancy and Henri Fiocca in the southern French port city of Marseille.

On October 16, an SS patrol burst into the house and detained Henri. The Nazis had mistaken him for the "White Mouse", never considering that the person they were looking for might actually be the wealthy industrialist's wife, Nancy Wake.

Fiocca was tortured for days before he died without ever confessing a single word. Meanwhile, Wake was ordered to flee, and she sought shelter in London.

SHE DID NOT FIND OUT THAT HER HUSBAND HAD BEEN KILLED UNTIL THE END OF THE WAR.

THE SS This paramilitary organization was formed in 1925 to be Hitler's bodyguards. As the importance of Nazism grew, they ended up having immense power.

REMARKABLE OPERATIONS

Once in the United Kingdom, the leader of the Resistance joined the Special Operations Executive (SOE) of the British army. It was in this secret organization that Wake trained in survival tactics and in handling radio transmitters.

APRIL 1944
MADAME ANDRÉE

On the night of April 29, 1944, Wake returned to occupied France and parachuted into the central Auvergne region. Her mission was to connect the British forces with the local guerrilla group led by Captain Tardivat. Her alias was Madame Andrée.

Wake managed to do this while leading sabotages and attacks against the Germans. Madame Andrée's cell blew up the arms storage facility at the Gestapo's headquarters in Montluçon, which was then successfully attacked.

DURING THE ATTACK, SHE KILLED ONE OF THE GERMAN ARMY GUARDS WHO DISCOVERED THEM AND TRIED TO REPORT THEM.

THE **OPERATIONS** OF NANCY WAKE'S SOE GROUP MOSTLY TOOK PLACE IN THE FRENCH DÉPARTEMENT OF ALLIER.

UNTIL LIBERATION
BIKE RIDE

From April 1944 until the liberation of Paris in August 1944, the 7,000 Resistance fighters led by Nancy Wake managed to control the 22,000 soldiers of the Third Reich. The French Resistance lost 100 men, but the German SS lost 14,000 soldiers..

When her Resistance group found itself without radio equipment in June 1944, Wake pedaled some 310 miles within 72 hours, dodging several Nazi checkpoints, to alert the London headquarters and obtain a replacement set.

HER COMPANIONS PRAISED HER BOLDNESS AND FIGHTING SPIRIT.

AFTER WORLD WAR II

After the war, Nancy Wake received a number of awards and honors from the Allied forces, including the Medal of Freedom from the United States and the Resistance Medal and Croix de Guerre ("War Cross") from France.

Many women risked their lives as messengers and radio operators from behind enemy lines, but there was only one who led such astonishingly large groups of men on the front line.

In the years that followed, Wake returned to Australia and ran for election with the Liberal Party. When she was not successful, she returned to the United Kingdom in 1951, working for the Intelligence Department of the British Air Ministry, where she taught her survival and escape skills and tactics.

In 1957, she married her second husband, John Melvin Forward, an Australian ex-combat pilot.

IN 1985, NANCY WAKE PUBLISHED HER AUTOBIOGRAPHY, *THE WHITE MOUSE*, WHICH WENT ON TO BECOME A BEST SELLER.

The Washington Post

FINAL

97th Year · · · · No. 222 · ·   AUGUST 10, 1974   Phone 223-6009   40¢

ANONYMOUS INFORMANT
UNCOVERS PRESIDENT NIXON'S SPY RING

MARK FELT, THE MYSTERIOUS FBI INFORMER KNOWN AS "DEEP THROAT."

THE WATERGATE SCANDAL PUT AN END TO THE POLITICAL CAREER OF US PRESIDENT RICHARD NIXON.

THE INFORMANT "DEEP THROAT" LEAKED INFORMATION TO THE PRESS ABOUT NIXON SPYING ON HIS DEMOCRATIC PARTY RIVALS.

NAME:	ALIAS:	BORN:	DEATH:	PROFILE:	CONFLICT:
WILLIAM MARK FELT	DEEP THROAT	AUGUST 17, 1913, IN TWIN FALLS, IDAHO, USA	DECEMBER 18, 2008, IN SANTA ROSA, CALIFORNIA, USA	FBI AGENT, INFORMER FOR *THE WASHINGTON POST* NEWSPAPER	THE WATERGATE SCANDAL

THE WATERGATE SCANDAL ERUPTS

AERIAL VIEW OF THE WATERGATE COMPLEX IN WASHINGTON, DC, WHERE THE US DEMOCRATIC PARTY'S OFFICES WERE LOCATED.

TWO HIGHLY INTUITIVE JOURNALISTS . . .

In the early hours of June 17, 1972, five people were arrested for trespassing and breaking into into the Democratic Party offices at the Watergate building in Washington, DC.

The case went unnoticed in the media, except by the young journalist Bob Woodward. As a reporter for *The Washington Post*, he personally attended the preliminary court hearing of the alleged small-time robbers who had been arrested at the Democratic Party offices.

Woodward was immediately alarmed when he learned that one of those arrested was James McCord, Jr., a former CIA agent. He was also intrigued to hear one of the others respond that they were "anticommunists" by profession.

The following day, Woodward and his colleague from *The Washington Post*, Carl Bernstein, published the following article in their newspaper: The two reporters suspected something of great importance was hidden behind the arrest and decided to start digging deeper.

> **The Washington Post**　　　　　　　　June 18, 1972
>
> Five men, one of whom said he is a former employee of the Central Intelligence Agency, were arrested at 2:30 a.m. yesterday in what authorities described as an elaborate plot to bug the offices of the Democratic National Committee here.

FORTUNATELY, A SECRET INFORMER WAS GOING TO HELP THEM A LOT WITH THEIR INVESTIGATIONS.

NIXON'S REACTION

Three days after the alleged criminal break-in to the Democratic Party's offices, President Nixon, a Republican, held a press conference washing his hands of the incident.

But the truth was very different: The US president threatened the arrested robbers and bought their silence by paying them large sums of money.

WOODWARD AND BERNSTEIN IN THE EDITORIAL DEPARTMENT OF *THE WASHINGTON POST* IN 1972.

THE MYSTERIOUS INFORMANT

The two journalists continued their investigations, and their collaboration with a front-line informer ended up being key. His identity stayed protected—he just went by the code name of "Deep Throat."

THE INFORMER WAS MARK FELT, THE FBI'S SECOND IN CHARGE, WHO WAS OVERSEEING THE WATERGATE CASE.

Because of his position, Felt wanted to avoid being linked to the reporter, and so he held secret meetings with him in a parking lot in the dead of night.

During his meetings with Bob Woodward, "Deep Throat" never actually provided any information; he only confirmed the veracity of the information presented to him by the journalist. He also guided Woodward in the investigation to ensure that the reporter remained on the right track.

The FBI informer advised *The Washington Post* reporter of the extreme measures the White House had taken to spy on its political opponents, journalists, and anyone else the government deemed "disloyal."

WOODWARD AND BERNSTEIN EVER CLOSER TO EXPOSING THE WATERGATE SCANDAL

1. THE FIVE PERSONS WHO WERE ARRESTED WERE NOT ROBBERS.

THE PRESIDENT'S SPIES

Those arrested turned out to be people trusted by Richard Nixon, in charge of resolving uncomfortable issues for the government. Their mission had been to install microphones in the Watergate building and tap the telephones of Nixon's political opponents to spy on them and secure the president's reelection.

They became known as the "plumbers" following their statement made to the police, "If they hired us to prevent leaks, it's because we're plumbers."

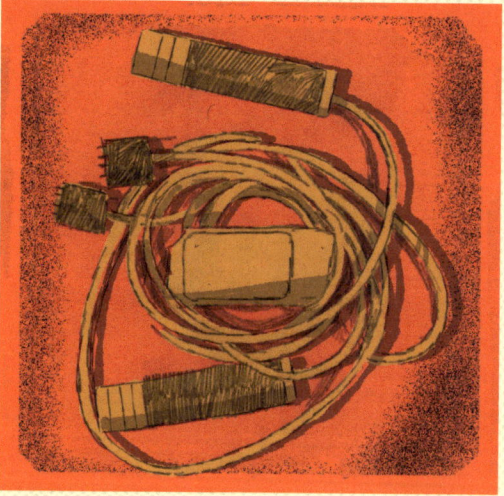

THE MICROPHONES THAT WERE INSTALLED IN THE DEMOCRATIC PARTY OFFICES IN THE WATERGATE BUILDING PROVIDED UNEQUIVOCAL PROOF THAT THE INTENTION HAD BEEN ESPIONAGE.

2. NIXON USED ILLEGAL FUNDS.

The two journalists discovered that a secret and illegal fund was being used to spy on and blackmail the Democrats and the president's enemies. It was controlled by the former head of the electoral campaign, John Mitchell, who had hastily resigned not long before.

IT WAS ALL PART OF AN ESPIONAGE AND SABOTAGE PLAN HATCHED TO ENSURE NIXON'S REELECTION.

NIXON IS REELECTED

Despite the revelations about the Watergate scandal that had been published by *The Washington Post*, Richard Nixon won a landslide victory over the Democratic Party candidate, Senator George McGovern, in the presidential elections on Tuesday, November 7, 1972.

THE REPUBLICAN PARTY

The Republicans consider themselves a center-right party focused on individual freedom and promotion of the free market. The Republicans tend to be more conservative than their Democrat rivals when it comes to social and national security matters.

THE DEMOCRATIC PARTY

The Democrats, on the other hand, consider themselves a center-left party. They focus on social equality, promoting civil rights, and protecting workers' rights.

NEW REVELATIONS IN THE WATERGATE CASE TRIAL

HIGH-RANKING OFFICIALS ARE FOUND TO BE INVOLVED.

Nixon's victory at the ballot boxes did not stop the fearless Woodward and Bernstein team from continuing their investigations while they were waiting for the trial of the accused.

It was once again McCord, the former CIA agent, who attracted everyone's attention by sending a letter to the judge. In it, he confessed that the five "plumbers" had been pressured and threatened to make them plead guilty.

He also explained that important and dangerous people were involved in the case, and if he revealed everything he knew, he would put his life at risk.

AFTER HEARING ABOUT THE LETTER, EVERYONE GOT INTERESTED IN THE CASE. *THE WASHINGTON POST* REPORTERS WERE NO LONGER ALONE.

THE CRISIS HITS THE WHITE HOUSE

The situation became untenable, and President Nixon was forced to lay off the government officials who had been smeared by the Watergate case.

This decision was not well received by those affected, and they took revenge on the president by revealing that Nixon always recorded the conversations held in the Oval Office, his main office, at the White House.

THE NIXON ADMINISTRATION FOUND ITSELF IN THE EYE OF THE STORM.

When this information came to light, the Supreme Court of the United States ordered President Nixon to hand over all the tapes he had made in order to include these as evidence in the Watergate trial.

After repeatedly refusing to provide the tapes to the Supreme Court, Nixon finally relented.

ONCE THE CONTENT OF THE TAPES BECAME KNOWN, IT SPARKED ONE OF THE BIGGEST POLITICAL SCANDALS IN US HISTORY.

A SERIOUS ESPIONAGE PLOT

THE RECORDINGS REVEAL THE WHITE HOUSE'S INVOLVEMENT IN THE WATERGATE SCANDAL.

The tapes of the recorded conversations held in the Watergate building revealed that President Nixon had not only been spying on the Democratic Party but that he had also tried to use the CIA to obstruct the FBI's investigation into the case.

A POLITICAL BOMBSHELL DROPS IN WASHINGTON!

Richard Nixon lost the support of his own Republican Party, which promptly initiated proceedings to remove him from office.

On August 9, 1974, the president announced his resignation to the astonished American people on television.

NIXON WAS THE FIRST US PRESIDENT EVER TO BE FORCED TO RESIGN FROM OFFICE.

INVESTIGATION

The scandal resulted in the imprisonment of various high-ranking White House officials. Nixon, on the other hand, never faced any charges because he was pardoned by Vice President Gerald Ford. This decision was controversial among Americans and cast a poor light on the trustworthiness of the system.

THE INFORMANT IS STILL IN HIDING.

Meanwhile, the FBI's second-in-command, Mark Felt, denied ever speaking with *The Washington Post* reporters. Only three decades later did Felt confess to being the mysterious "faceless" informer known to all as "Deep Throat."

The courageous reporters Bob Woodward and Carl Bernstein received the prestigious Pulitzer Prize in journalism and demonstrated the importance of independent investigative journalism as a control mechanism in democracies.

"TO LEAVE OFFICE BEFORE MY TERM IS COMPLETED IS ABHORRENT TO EVERY INSTINCT IN MY BODY. BUT AS PRESIDENT, I MUST PUT THE INTEREST OF AMERICA FIRST," NIXON STATED DURING HIS TELEVISED MESSAGE ANNOUNCING HIS RESIGNATION.

CITIZENS READING THE NEWS OUTSIDE THE WHITE HOUSE ON THE DAY OF PRESIDENT NIXON'S RESIGNATION. IT WAS THE ONLY THING PEOPLE TALKED ABOUT.

Cambridge  Daily News

SUNDAY, NOVEMBER 11, 1990

THE CAMBRIDGE FIVE

IN THE 1930S, FIVE BRITISH UNIVERSITY STUDENTS WERE RECRUITED BY THE SOVIET UNION AS SPIES.

THEY WERE FAR-LEFT INTELLECTUALS WHO PASSED ON CLASSIFIED INFORMATION FOR DECADES BEFORE BEING DISCOVERED.

THEIR EXPOSURE SPARKED A MAJOR SCANDAL IN THE UNITED KINGDOM.

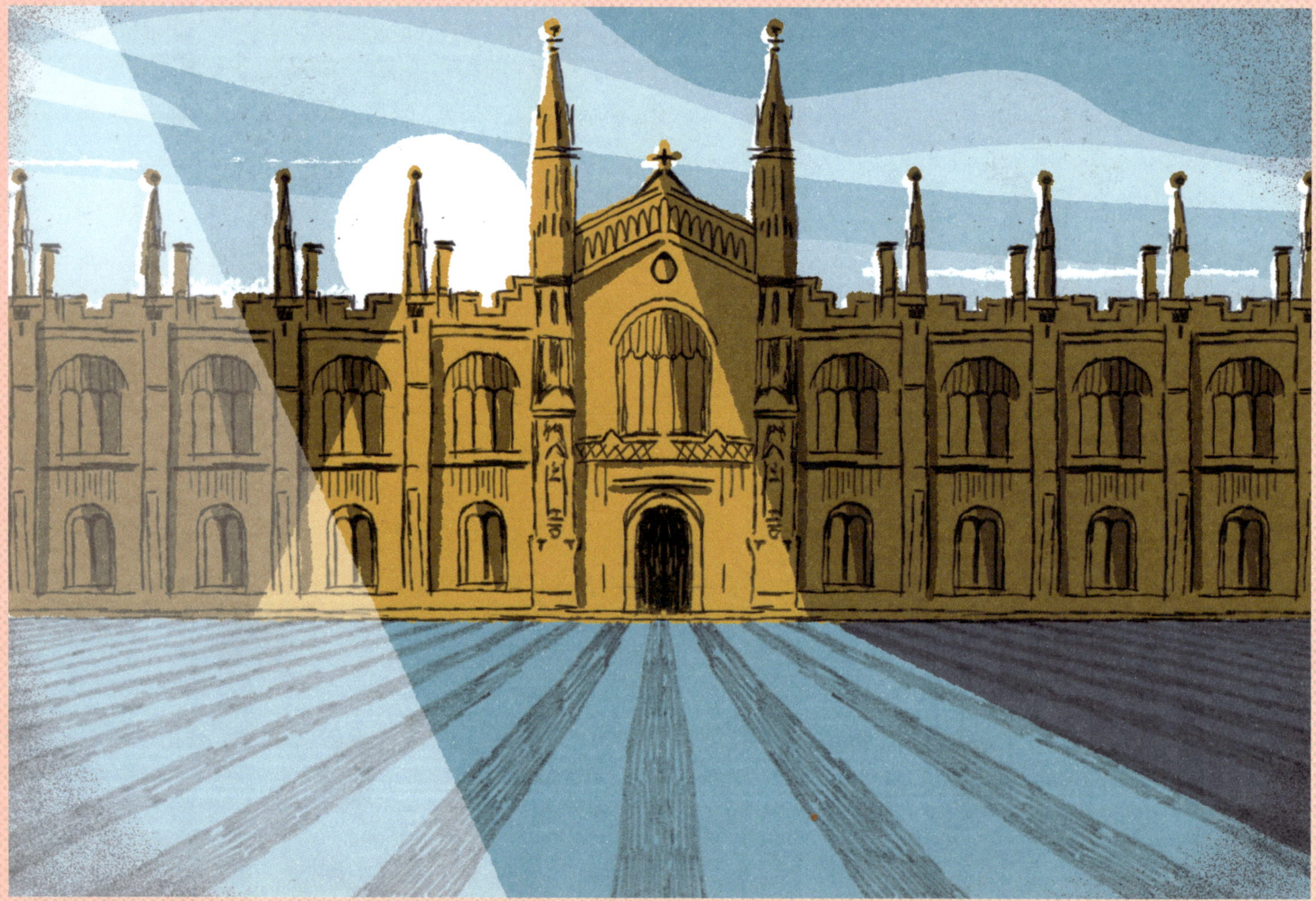

THE MAIN FAÇADE OF CORPUS CHRISTI COLLEGE AT CAMBRIDGE UNIVERSITY, ONE OF THE OLDEST AND MOST PRESTIGIOUS IN THE WORLD.

NAMES:	ALIAS:	CREATED:	PROFILE:	CONFLICT:
KIM PHILBY, DONALD MACLEAN, GUY BURGESS, ANTHONY BLUNT AND JOHN CAIRNCROSS	THE CAMBRIDGE FIVE (OR SPY CIRCLE)	IN THE MID-1930S	BRITISH STUDENTS WITH IMPECCABLE ACADEMIC RECORDS	INTERWAR EUROPE, WORLD WAR II, AND THE COLD WAR

COMMUNISTS WANTED

In the 1930s, fascism was on the rise in Europe, and many students joined communist parties as a means of fighting against it.

The Soviets took advantage of the situation to secure young communists and turn them into spies. The NKVD, its secret service, was in charge of recruiting the Cambridge Five.

THE STRATEGY OF THE SOVIETS WAS TO RECRUIT BRIGHT EUROPEAN STUDENTS WHO WERE COMMUNISTS.

THE SOVIET INTELLIGENCE SERVICES

It was the role of the People's Commissariat for Internal Affairs (NKVD) to maintain the Soviet Union's security. This authority sent out secret agents to obtain confidential information, control citizens' uprisings, and monitor political dissidents. It also recruited potential spies in other countries.

THE SOVIET PLAN, STEP BY STEP

1. FIVE NEW STUDENTS ARRIVE AT CAMBRIDGE UNIVERSITY.

Kim Philby, Donald Maclean, Guy Burgess, and Anthony Blunt started their studies at Cambridge, one of the most famous and respected universities in the UK, between 1929 and 1931. John Cairncross followed suit a little later.

THEY WERE INTELLIGENT YOUNG MEN CONCERNED ABOUT THE RISE OF FASCISM. MOST CAME FROM WEALTHY, HIGHLY ESTEEMED FAMILIES. THEY WERE THE PERFECT CANDIDATES FOR MOSCOW AND WERE TARGETED BY THE NKVD.

2. THE RECRUITMENT PROCESS

Arnold Deutsch, one of Moscow's agent recruiters, traveled to the UK. He approached the students at meetings held by the Cambridge Apostles, a secret society to which they belonged.

THE FIVE GOT TO WORK AS SPIES FOR THE SOVIETS.

3. GRADUATION WITH HONORS

The newly recruited students graduated from Cambridge University with excellent grades and joined Britain's social elite.

Following orders from Moscow, the young men stopped publicly expressing their communist ideas and views.

4. ENTRY INTO GOVERNMENT

With their brilliant academic records, good reputations, and excellent contacts, it wasn't hard for the graduates to find work and climb the ranks within the Foreign Office and other governmental departments.

5. SENDING REPORTS

From their new positions, the agents would periodically send reports to the Soviet Union, and these proved to be even more valuable once World War II began in 1939.

THE FIVE "MOLES" HAD INFILTRATED THE BRITISH INTELLIGENCE SERVICE AND PLAYED A KEY ROLE FOR THE SOVIETS.

WORLD WAR AND COLD WAR

World War II (1939–1945) pitted the Axis powers (Nazi Germany, fascist Italy, the Japanese Empire) against the Allies (United Kingdom, Soviet Union, the United States, France). This bloody conflict was followed by the Cold War, a clash between the realigned sides—the capitalist bloc, which was led by the United States, and the communist bloc, headed by the Soviet Union.

THE DAMAGE CAUSED BY THE CAMBRIDGE FIVE DURING WORLD WAR II AND THE COLD WAR IS IMMEASURABLE.

MOLE
This term is used colloquially to denote an agent who has infiltrated an organization to obtain information.

THE CAMBRIDGE FIVE

DONALD MACLEAN

GUY BURGESS

KIM PHILBY

ANTHONY BLUNT

JOHN CAIRNCROSS

THE FIVE SPIES WERE CONVINCED THAT SOVIET COMMUNISM WAS THE BEST POSSIBLE POLITICAL SYSTEM AND, ABOVE ALL, THAT IT WAS THE BEST DEFENSE AGAINST FASCISM.

KIM PHILBY  (1912–1988)

THE MOST FAMOUS MEMBER OF THE GROUP AND CONSIDERED TO BE THE BEST SPY IN HISTORY.

ALIAS:
STANLEY

BORN:
1912 IN INDIA, WHERE HIS FATHER, A BRITISH ARMY OFFICER, WAS BASED

PROFILE:
JOURNALIST, MEMBER OF BRITAIN'S MI6, AND SOVIET DOUBLE AGENT

REMARKABLE MISSIONS

Philby managed to rise rapidly up the ranks and become one of the most notable members of the Britain's secret intelligence service while also working as a spy for the Soviets.

Toward the end of World War II, he was appointed Head of Counterespionage at MI6 (the United Kingdom's foreign intelligence service). While active in this role, he managed to protect his four Cambridge classmates.

PHILBY OUTWITTED BRITISH INTELLIGENCE AND MANAGED TO KEEP HIS IDENTITY SECRET.

In 1949, he was based in Washington, DC, as the main intermediary between British intelligence and the CIA. During his years of service, he leaked valuable information from British intelligence, revealing to the Soviets the identities of British and American secret agents who had infiltrated the KGB (the Soviet Committee for State Security).

DOZENS OF BRITISH AND AMERICAN SPIES WERE DISCOVERED, THANKS TO INFORMATION FROM KIM PHILBY.

In 1951, Philby helped two of his former Cambridge classmates, Donald Maclean and Guy Burgess, to escape to the Soviet Union after they had been discovered.

LUCK RUNS OUT

Donald Maclean's and Guy Burgess's exposure and escape left Kim Philby vulnerable. From that moment on, the British secret service started seriously investigating him.

THE KGB GAVE HIM THE OPTION OF "DISAPPEARING OFF THE MAP," BUT PHILBY REFUSED TO FLEE AND DECIDED TO "PROVE HIS INNOCENCE."

In December 1961, a new investigation led to the revelation of his treason. Philby escaped to Moscow and was promoted to the rank of KGB general. He died at his home in Moscow on May 11, 1988.

DONALD MACLEAN (1913–1983)

THE ATOMIC AGENT OF CAMBRIDGE

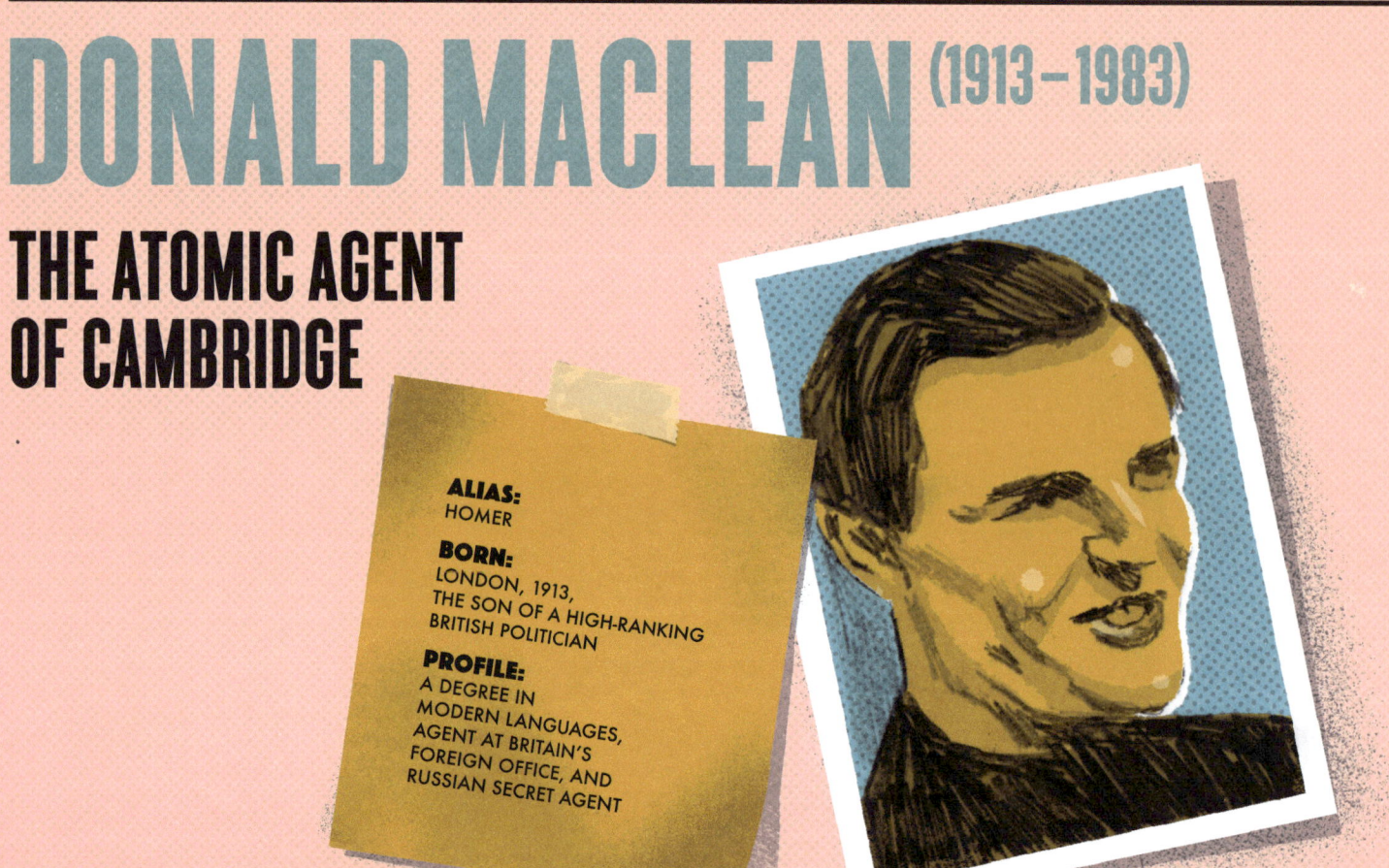

ALIAS:
HOMER

BORN:
LONDON, 1913,
THE SON OF A HIGH-RANKING
BRITISH POLITICIAN

PROFILE:
A DEGREE IN
MODERN LANGUAGES,
AGENT AT BRITAIN'S
FOREIGN OFFICE, AND
RUSSIAN SECRET AGENT

NUCLEAR INFORMATION

In 1934, Donald Maclean started working for the British Foreign Office. While based at the British embassy in Paris, he sent detailed reports containing sensitive information to the Soviet authorities.

A few years later, he was promoted and sent to another British embassy, this time in Washington, DC. In the United States, he sat on the multilateral committee for nuclear energy and the development of atomic weapons. Maclean sent all the classified reports to the Soviet Union.

HE WAS ONE OF THE MOST IMPORTANT ATOMIC SPIES OF THE 20TH CENTURY.

ESCAPE TO MOSCOW

In 1951, the British agents working on the Venona Project, a United States counter-intelligence program, found out that Maclean was spying for the Soviets.

Burgess, his university contemporary from Cambridge, warned Maclean of his imminent arrest, and the pair escaped together to Moscow with the help of Kim Philby and Anthony Blunt.

In the Soviet Union, Maclean was decorated by the KGB, where he also worked as a foreign policy adviser. His wife, Melinda, who knew about his double life, and their three children joined him two years later.

Maclean died in Moscow in March 1983.

THE VENONA PROJECT

This was the name of the United States counterintelligence program that decoded some 3,000 secret Soviet messages. It led to the discovery of the Cambridge Five spy ring in the United Kingdom and other Moscow-based operations.

GUY BURGESS (1911–1963)

THE INTELLECTUAL AND ARISTOCRATIC SPY

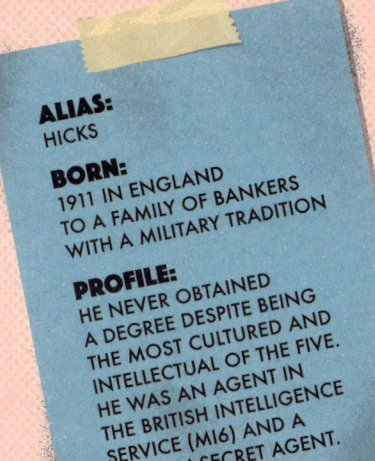

ALIAS:
HICKS

BORN:
1911 IN ENGLAND TO A FAMILY OF BANKERS WITH A MILITARY TRADITION

PROFILE:
HE NEVER OBTAINED A DEGREE DESPITE BEING THE MOST CULTURED AND INTELLECTUAL OF THE FIVE. HE WAS AN AGENT IN THE BRITISH INTELLIGENCE SERVICE (MI6) AND A RUSSIAN SECRET AGENT.

PRIVILEGED POSITIONS

In 1935, Guy Burgess left Cambridge University and, following orders from Moscow, publicly denounced communism. He began to work at the BBC, Britain's public radio broadcaster, where he forged contacts with influential figures from the cultural and political scenes.

Just before the outbreak of World War II, Burgess secured a position in the British secret intelligence service. By the end of World War II, he was already working at the Foreign Affairs Press Department, where he was in charge of advising the foreign editors and diplomats of the United Kingdom's political decisions—a privileged position for a spy.

In 1947, he worked at the British embassy in Washington, DC—a role that gave him access to valuable internal material that he would systematically send to Moscow.

> DURING HIS TIME IN WASHINGTON, DC, BURGESS WOULD SPEND HIS EVENINGS PHOTOGRAPHING IMPORTANT DOCUMENTS THAT HE WOULD THEN LEAK TO THE KGB.

ESCAPE WITH MACLEAN

In 1951, Burgess warned his comrade Maclean of his imminent arrest, and the pair escaped to Moscow with Philby's assistance.

Burgess never adapted to his new life behind the Iron Curtain. He never learned Russian, nor did he obtain Soviet citizenship.

As a gay man, he also had to hide his sexuality because of the savage way this would have been punished by the communist authorities. He died in 1963, likely due to his problem with alcohol.

ANTHONY BLUNT (1907–1983)

ROYAL ART CURATOR AND SPY

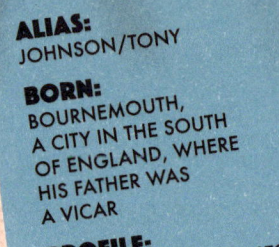

ALIAS:
JOHNSON/TONY

BORN:
BOURNEMOUTH,
A CITY IN THE SOUTH
OF ENGLAND, WHERE
HIS FATHER WAS
A VICAR

PROFILE:
PROFESSOR OF ART HISTORY
AND CURATOR OF THE BRITISH
ROYAL ART COLLECTION,
BRITISH SECRET
SERVICE (MI5) AGENT,
RUSSIAN SPY

THE FOURTH MAN

Following a trip to Moscow and with Guy Burgess's influence, Blunt was recruited by the Soviet NKVD while at Cambridge.

In 1940, he was recruited by the British secret service (MI5) and passed on information to Moscow. Blunt had access to secret information obtained by the British agents spying on the Nazis.

Blunt was a member of the United Kingdom's high society, and his contacts with top politicians were very useful to him when reporting British secrets to the Soviet Union.

In 1945, he was hired as the royal art curator and stopped working as a spy, though he did help Burgess and Maclean escape from the United Kingdom in 1951.

ONE OF HIS GREAT ACHIEVEMENTS WAS HIS RECOVERY OF A SERIES OF LETTERS THE DUKE OF WINDSOR HAD WRITTEN TO HITLER AND OTHER NAZI LEADERS.

* * *

IN 1956, HE WAS KNIGHTED BY THE QUEEN.

AN OBSCURE CASE

In 1964, Michael Straight, an American Anthony Blunt had tried to recruit, denounced him. Finally, the secret service knew the identity of the fourth spy of the Cambridge Circle. He avoided prison in exchange for collaborating with them.

Because of his status as a knight, his case never came to light, even 15 years later. In 1979, the decision was made to dismiss him from his role as royal art curator and strip him of his knighthood. In his memoirs, Blunt stated that spying for the Soviets was the worst mistake of his life. He died of a heart attack in London at the age of 75.

JOHN CAIRNCROSS (1913–1995)

THE MYSTERIOUS "FIFTH MAN" OF THE CAMBRIDGE SPY CIRCLE

ALIAS:
THE FIFTH MAN/LISZT

HIS IDENTITY WAS THE SUBJECT OF SPECULATION FOR DECADES.

BORN:
1913 IN SCOTLAND
HE WAS THE SON OF A HARDWARE STORE OWNER AND A TEACHER.

PROFILE:
A SCHOLARSHIP STUDENT, NOT FROM THE UPPER CLASSES LIKE HIS COMPANIONS, CIVIL SERVANT AT THE FOREIGN OFFICE, AND RUSSIAN SECRET AGENT

INVESTIGATION
THE "MOLE" HUNT

Among the messages that the Venona Project was able to decode, the United Kingdom noted the presence of Soviet moles within the ranks of its top government leaders.

Prime Minister Margaret Thatcher launched a thorough investigation during the course of which the service managed to hunt down and gradually expose each one of the spy circle's elusive members.

The operation ended in 1979 when the identity of the "fifth man" was revealed.

THE DISMANTLING OF THE CAMBRIDGE SPY CIRCLE MARRED THE IMPECCABLE REPUTATION OF BRITISH HIGH SOCIETY.

BOMB SECRETS

As a German translator, he deciphered and leaked Nazi war messages coded with the Enigma machine.

THE ENIGMA MACHINE

This was a cipher device used by the German intelligence service and military. While the coding was considered to be virtually unbreakable, the Allies still managed to decipher some of the coded messages.

Cairncross worked in the Secret Intelligence Service (also known as MI6) and had access to the Manhattan Project, a top-secret program to build atomic bombs.

FOR MORE THAN A DECADE, CAIRNCROSS SUPPLIED THE SOVIET INTELLIGENCE WITH THOUSANDS OF DOCUMENTS ON THE ANGLO-AMERICAN PROJECT TO CREATE THE ATOMIC BOMB.

FINALLY DISCOVERED

In 1951, once Donald Maclean and Guy Burgess had escaped to the Soviet Union to avoid capture, some notes written by Cairncross were found in Burgess's home, and the British intelligence service interrogated him.

CAIRNCROSS RESIGNED FROM HIS POSITION BUT WAS ABLE TO GO INTO EXILE.

A KGB defector confirmed his existence in 1990. In 1995, Cairncross returned to England, where he died six months later.

Neues Deutschland

Sozialistische Tageszeitung

Berlin Edition "Vorwärts" — Berlin, Thursday, September 26, 1991 — Year 46 / No. 230 (daily expt. on Sundays)

MARKUS WOLF

AND HIS GROUP OF "ROMEO SPIES"

WOLF INFILTRATED AGENTS INTO WEST GERMANY WHO WERE SPECIALIZED IN SEDUCING WOMEN.

MARKUS WOLF WAS A MAESTRO OF ESPIONAGE IN THE FORMER EAST GERMANY (THE GDR, OR GERMAN DEMOCRATIC REPUBLIC). WITHIN THE INTELLIGENCE AGENCIES OF WESTERN COUNTRIES, HE WAS KNOWN AS "THE MAN WITHOUT A FACE," BECAUSE FOR MANY YEARS, NO ONE KNEW WHAT HE LOOKED LIKE.

NAME:	ALIAS:	BORN:	PROFILE:	CONFLICT:	DEATH:
MARKUS JOHANNES WOLF	"THE MAN WITHOUT A FACE", "ROMEO SPY"	JANUARY 19, 1923, HECHINGEN, GERMANY	HEAD OF THE GDR'S SECRET SERVICE (STASI) ABROAD	THE COLD WAR	NOVEMBER 9, 2006, IN BERLIN, GERMANY

A COMMUNIST JEWISH FAMILY

Markus was the son of a Jewish doctor, Friedrich Wolf, who was a member of the German Communist Party. His mother, Else, was a teacher and also a communist.

The year 1933, when Adolf Hitler came to power in Germany, marked the start of increasingly savage persecutions of Jews, communists, and other groups targeted by the Nazis. The Wolf family, like many others, were forced to flee the country, and they settled in the Soviet Union.

Young Markus studied at the Moscow Institute of Aircraft Engineering, and he later worked as an editor of a communist publication.

BETWEEN 1933 AND 1945, HITLER EXECUTED MILLIONS OF PEOPLE — JEWS, POLES AND SOVIETS, THE DISABLED, GYPSIES, POLITICAL DISSIDENTS ...

A YOUNG MARKUS WOLF, SHOWN BETWEEN HIS BROTHER, KONRAD, AND HIS FATHER, FRIEDRICH WOLF, A VERY ACTIVE, DIE-HARD COMMUNIST.

A DIVIDED GERMANY

Following the Third Reich's defeat at the end of World War II, Germany found itself divided into four occupied territories: the American, British, French, and Soviet zones of occupation.

In 1949, three of these zones united to form the Federal Republic of Germany or BRD (West Germany), while the Soviet zone became the German Democratic Republic, or GDR (East Germany).

The two Germanys had very different political and economic systems. The West adopted a democratic, capitalist system, and the East an authoritarian, communist system.

THE NUREMBERG TRIALS

In the German city of Nuremberg, an international tribunal, made up of representatives of the Allied nations, tried and sentenced the leading Nazi officials for war crimes and crimes against peace and humanity.

ACCUSED NAZIS IN THE DOCK IN NUREMBERG, SEPTEMBER 30, 1946.

RETURNING HOME

After World War II ended, Markus Wolf was able to return from exile and settle in Germany's Soviet-occupied zone.

There he spent the first year working at a radio station under the pseudonym of Michael Storm, reporting on the rulings from the Nuremberg Trials against the leading Nazis.

HEAD OF THE SECRET SERVICE

In 1953, Wolf joined East Germany's newly formed intelligence service, the Ministry for State Security *(Staatssicherheitsdienst)* or Stasi for short.

He soon became one of the top bosses of the German Democratic Republic's spy organization.

His main task was to infiltrate spies into West Germany—into ministries, embassies, and military barracks on the other side of the Berlin Wall.

The Stasi agents would be equipped with a range of very effective espionage tools.

WOLF WAS CONSIDERED ONE OF THE STASI'S MASTER SPIES.

THE STASI

East Germany's secret police and intelligence organization spied and monitored its citizens through a vast network of secret agents and informers. It also established a very effective international espionage system.

HIDDEN CAMERAS

The Stasi were the undisputed experts at designing spy devices. Its agents hid cameras in everyday objects that raised no suspicion. This enabled them to take photographs undetected.

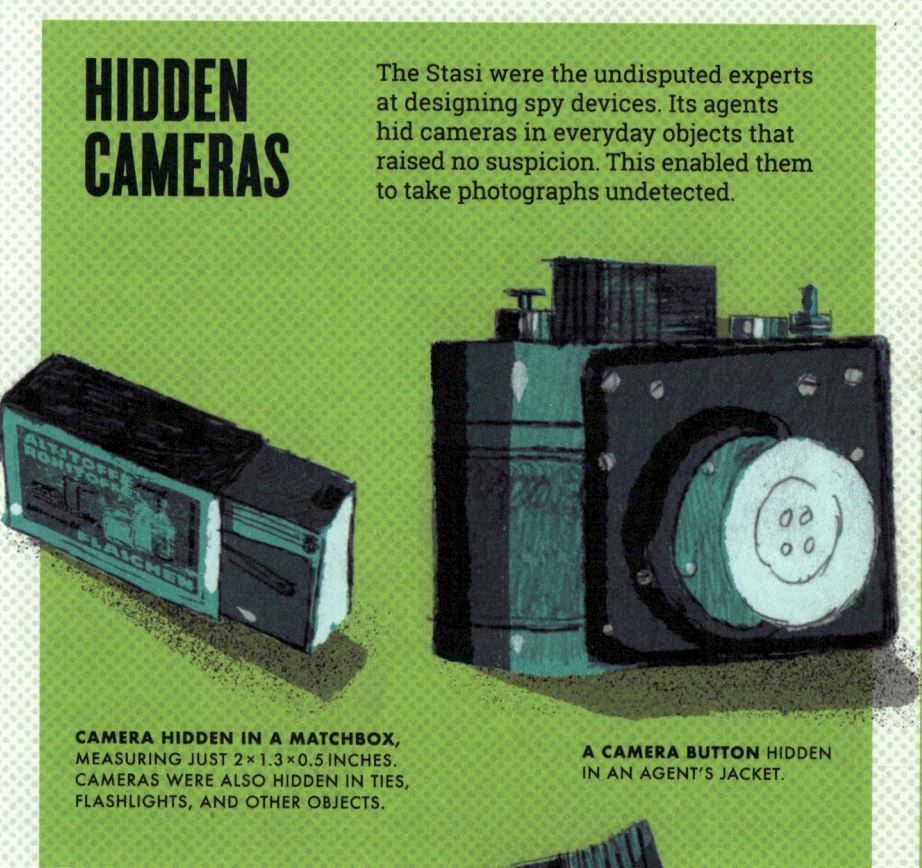

CAMERA HIDDEN IN A MATCHBOX, MEASURING JUST 2 × 1.3 × 0.5 INCHES. CAMERAS WERE ALSO HIDDEN IN TIES, FLASHLIGHTS, AND OTHER OBJECTS.

A CAMERA BUTTON HIDDEN IN AN AGENT'S JACKET.

THE SYMBOL OF EAST GERMANY'S *STAATSSICHERHEITSDIENST* (STATE SECURITY SERVICE), KNOWN UNIVERSALLY AS THE STASI.

LONG-RANGE CAMERAS

The agents had cameras with telephoto lenses. This technology enabled them to take photographs of people from very far away, without any fear of being discovered.

REFLEX CAMERA FITTED WITH A 300-MM SUPER-TELEPHOTO LENS.

SECRET DEVICES TO TRANSMIT INFORMATION

The agents had objects that would fit in their bags without attracting attention and which had secret compartments in which they could hide microfilms and any kind of secret information they managed to obtain.

A GERMAN FIVE-MARK COIN (DATING FROM THE 1970S) WAS ADAPTED TO CONTAIN A MICROFILM.

HIDDEN WEAPONS

Other resources used by the Stasi included weapons hidden in such a way that they did not need to be pulled out to be fired, such as this machine gun fitted into a briefcase.

THE ŠKORPION MACHINE GUN WEIGHED ONLY THREE POUNDS WHEN FULLY LOADED.

THE "ROMEO SPIES" NETWORK

Wolf devised a clever strategy to infiltrate agents into West Germany. He created a special group of male spies trained to seduce female workers who held powerful positions in West Germany and obtain information from them. It was called a network of "Romeo spies."

WOLF BELIEVED HE COULD OBTAIN MORE INFORMATION FROM A SECRETARY THAN FROM TOP OFFICERS.

PROFILE:

The agents were handsome men, usually around forty years old.

STRATEGY:

1.
The spies knew all about the women they targeted. They went after those who were heartbroken as a result of a break-up or the loss of their loved one. They played on the women's emotions.

2.
They had to gain the women's trust, and once they had strong emotional ties, the spies started to request secret information.

3.
Some even married their victims to get a stronger hold on them should they discover their husbands' true identity.

VICTIMS OF THE "ROMEOS"

MARGARETHE LUBIG

Margarethe Lubig worked as a secretary in the West German Ministry of Defense when she was seduced by Roland Gandt, a Danish agent pretending to be a journalist.

The Casanova sourced information from Margarethe for 25 of the 28 years that Germany was divided.

MARGARETHE SUPPLIED HIM WITH THE MOST VALUABLE NATO DOCUMENTS OF THE LAST 30 YEARS.

ROLAND GANDT CAREFULLY STUDIED MARGARETHE'S HABITS AND CHARACTER TRAITS FOR MONTHS IN ORDER TO WIN HER OVER.

GABRIELE KLIEM

Gabriele Kliem was a translator and interpreter working at the US embassy in Bonn (the capital of West Germany at the time). She could never have imagined that her boyfriend was really a Stasi spy. A tall, handsome, blond haired, blue-eyed man, he first investigated her private life before approaching her in one of the city's parks.

She was waiting for a friend when, Dietzel, Wolf's Romeo, introduced himself, apologizing for his "sick colleague" and offering to take her to dinner instead.

GABRIELE KLIEM SPENT SEVEN YEARS COMMITTED TO THE "MAN OF HER DREAMS," WHO WAS ACTUALLY A STASI AGENT.

DAGMAR KAHLIG-SCHEFFLER

Dagmar Kahlig-Scheffler was the personal secretary of Chancellor Helmut Schmidt. The Romeo who seduced her was one of the Stasi's great stars: Hans Stöhler. This agent was a former pilot who pretended to be a real estate agent. He managed to obtain valuable notes that Dagmar would take during her boss's conversations with top anti-Soviet political leaders.

DAGMAR WAS FOUND OUT, ARRESTED, AND SENTENCED TO FOUR AND A HALF YEARS IN PRISON.

DAGMAR KAHLIG-SCHEFFLER GETTING OFF THE PRISON BUS UNDER THE SUPERVISION OF TWO POLICE OFFICERS WHO TOOK HER TO THE COURT HEARING IN DÜSSELDORF ON OCTOBER 4, 1978.

HELEN ANDERSON

This young Englishwoman was working at an American base in Berlin. Her Romeo, Dietmar Schumacher, convinced her to steal various classified files from NATO.

Including Helen Anderson, there were some 40-odd women victims who fell for the charms of Markus Wolf's Romeo spies and who were eventually discovered and tried for espionage in West Germany.

END OF OPERATIONS

Wolf managed to keep his identity secret for decades, which is why he became known as the Cold War's "man without a face."

IN THE WEST, NOBODY KNEW WHO HE WAS OR WHAT HE LOOKED LIKE.

In 1978, his face ceased to be a mystery when he was caught on camera by a photographer in Sweden. Nearly a decade later, at the age of 63, Wolf retired and devoted himself to writing his memoirs, which included the notable work *Man Without a Face*.

CONVICTED

Following Germany's reunification in 1991, and having been denied political asylum by his government, Wolf fled to the Soviet Union.

In 1991, he turned himself in to the federal German authorities. He was tried and convicted through various proceedings in his country, but he never went to prison; he could not be executed in the Federal Republic of Germany for being a spy in the former East Germany.

THE SPY WITHOUT A FACE WENT UNPUNISHED.

KEPT SECRETS

Wolf died in his sleep at home in Berlin on November 9, 2006, at the age of 83, taking some secrets with him to the grave. He is buried alongside his brother, Konrad.

KONRAD WOLF
1925 – 1982
MARKUS WOLF
1923 – 2006

MARKUS "MISHA" WOLF, SEEN HERE IN THE VICINITY OF THE BRANDENBURG GATE IN BERLIN IN 1991, TWO YEARS AFTER THE FALL OF THE WALL IN THE GERMAN CAPITAL.